Z

GW00670538

Zany Buildings

Sometimes architects think outside the box. Here are some of the more 'zany' experiments of modern architecture that can be found in town.

St John's Church, Broadbridge Heath

Opened in the early 1960s after replacing an older Edwardian church, its pyramid-like shape consists of four large triangular vertical façades, joined at the centre and tiled down to ground level between each triangle. It is certainly a unique design, nestled within the residential streets of Broadbridge Heath.

Law Courts, Hurst Road

Perhaps one of the least attractive buildings that can be found in Horsham, the law courts were clearly designed for function rather than appearance. Resembling a kind of modern-day castle, visitors cross a bridge over the 'moat' (the car park), through a gateway bearing a large royal coat of arms and into a central courtyard. Behind the courts is the police station, which moved here from Barttelot Road. The current station retains the red lantern from the old station.

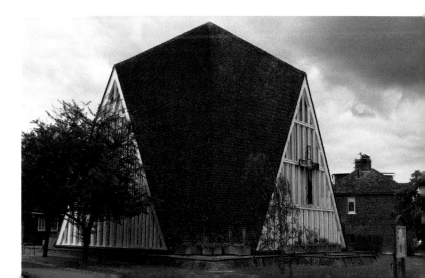

St John's Church, Broadbridge Heath.

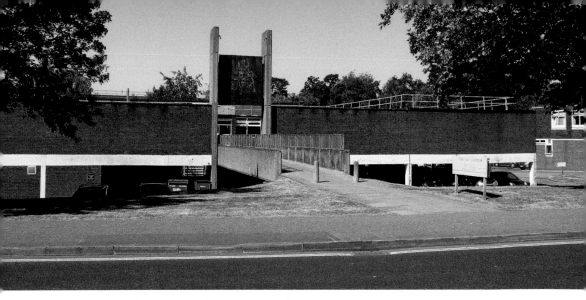

The Law Courts in Hurst Road. A modern castle?

West Point, Springfield Road

Perhaps one of the most unusual buildings in Horsham, along with St John's Church at Broadbridge Heath, West Point is certainly a statement piece in the centre of town. Each floor of its five storeys is rotated at 45° to the one below, creating a star-shaped profile from above. Even the stairwell on the southern side of the building includes this offset design of each floor, resembling a Jenga block tower. West Point is definitely a unique feature on Horsham's landscape.

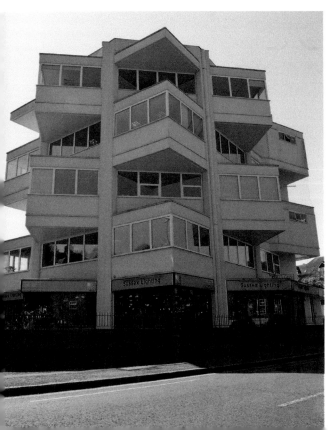

West Point, Springfield Road.

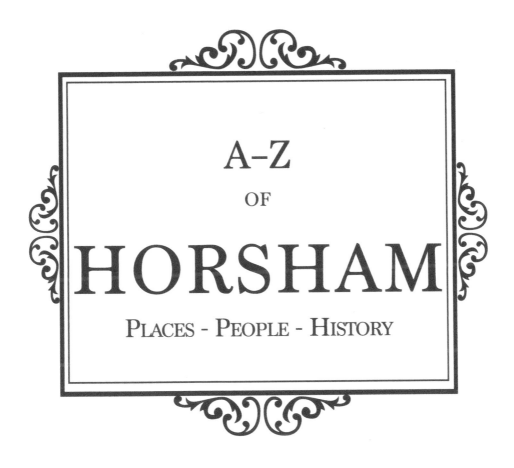

A–Z

OF

HORSHAM

PLACES - PEOPLE - HISTORY

Eddy Greenfield

AMBERLEY

First published 2019

Amberley Publishing
The Hill, Stroud, Gloucestershire, GL5 4EP
www.amberley-books.com

Copyright © Eddy Greenfield, 2019

The right of Eddy Greenfield to be identified
as the Author of this work has been asserted in
accordance with the Copyrights, Designs and
Patents Act 1988.

ISBN 978 1 4456 8631 8 (print)
ISBN 978 1 4456 8632 5 (ebook)

British Library Cataloguing in Publication Data.
A catalogue record for this book is available from
the British Library.

Origination by Amberley Publishing.
Printed in Great Britain.

Contents

Introduction

An author's own tastes and interests will have a bearing on what facts and figures are included in their work; something that may not be of interest to them is unlikely to be included. The same is true of this book, which can only ever aim to provide little more than a glimpse into the long and fascinating history of the town. Therefore, I have aimed to present some of the lesser-known and more unusual history that I have unearthed. Some familiar landmarks will be explored, as will famous (and infamous) inhabitants, the town's military heritage and the darkness that almost gripped Horsham in the 1930s.

The hardest thing about writing this book was deciding what to include within the space available, since most of the chapters are worthy of being a book in their own right. I have therefore opted to expend greater detail on some chapters that I think most readers will find particularly interesting, or that are perhaps less known about. I hope that I have managed to strike the right balance.

Included are tales of crime, cruel punishments, plague, murder, war and witchcraft, and it should be questioned whether these events can be considered 'entertainment'. I would not consider them to be so, but rather they are interesting incidents in the long history of Horsham that have shaped the town we know today. It should be remembered that these events all involved real people, with families of their own.

I hope, very much, that you will enjoy this latest addition to Horsham's written history and that you uncover one or two surprises along the way!

Lastly, I wish to give special thanks and acknowledgement to Gary Shipton, editor of the *West Sussex County Times*, for his kind permission to use two images from the newspaper.

Horsham – a town nestled in the Sussex Weald.

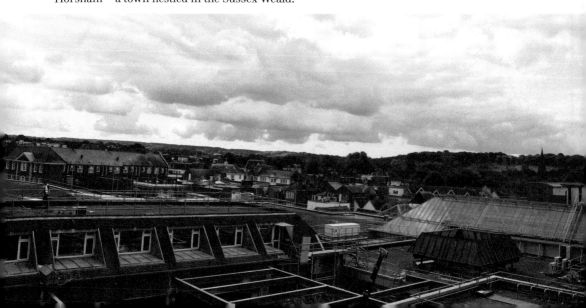

Acid Bath Murders

Perhaps better known for his links to Crawley, where his workshop at No. 2 Leopold Road was located, Horsham played a key role in the story of John George Haigh – better known to history as the Acid Bath Murderer. It was shortly after murdering and dissolving in acid the body of his sixth and final victim, Olive Durand-Deacon, that Haigh visited Walter Bull & Sons Jewellers at No. 9 Middle Street to sell jewellery that he recovered from her body. It was this act that ultimately led to his downfall, since it was Mr Bull who identified Haigh to the police as being the man who sold him the items.

No. 9 Middle Street, formerly Walter Bull & Sons Jewellers.

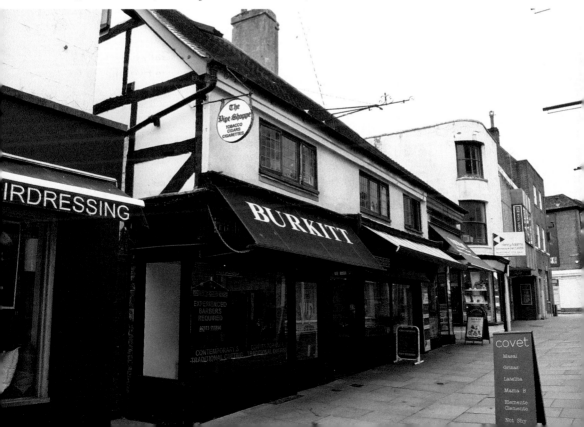

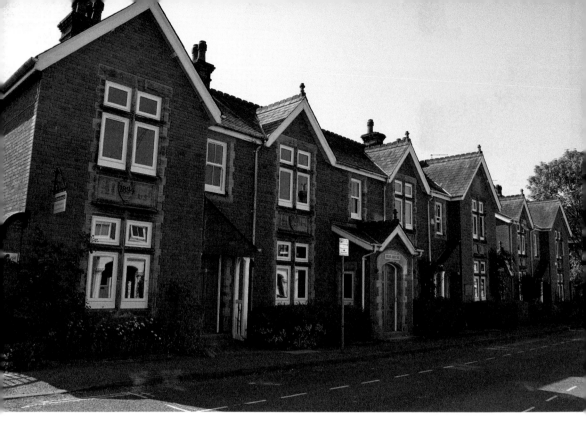

The former police station in Barttelot Road.

After his arrest in 1949, he was incarcerated in Cell No. 2 of the Barttelot Road police station for the duration of his initial trial at Horsham Magistrates Court, which at the time was in the Old Town Hall. It was whilst held at Horsham that Haigh claimed he was a vampire who drank the blood of his victims in a failed attempt to plead insanity and avoid the death penalty. At each of his five hearings at the town hall before the trial moved to Lewes, Market Square was packed full of people eager to catch a glimpse of the celebrity criminal as he entered and exited the court via the external steps at the rear of the building.

Horsham Museum has on display the original door to Cell No. 2 and a comb Haigh used while imprisoned in Lewes.

Anchor Hotel

Almost beside the Old Town Hall stands the Anchor Hotel. The present decorative façade of the building bears the date 1899, though a hotel on the site dates back much earlier. It is from this hotel that, on 30 September 1861, Mr Elson commenced the task of walking 60 miles a day for six days. On each day he set off from the Anchor at 6.00 a.m. to the Fox Inn at Three Bridges (now The Snooty Fox) and then back again, walking through all the main roads and highways in Horsham on the way in order to make up 20 miles. He would repeat each journey three times a day.

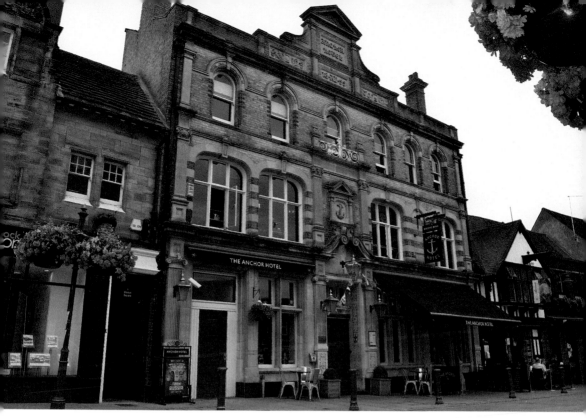

The Anchor Hotel in Market Square.

This was not the first, nor the last, time that Horsham had seen such walking feats. In 1826, William Verrall walked 50 miles a day for twenty days, and on 5 January 1889 a lady began her attempt to walk 50 miles in just twelve hours in a repeating course along East Street, around the Carfax and along West Street. This latter effort was in benefit of charity, though the reason behind the other two events remains a mystery.

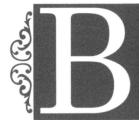

Bax Holmes and the Horshamosaurus

Born in 1803 in Horsham and spending much of his life living in The Causeway, George Bax Holmes became best known for his discovery of fossils in the Horsham area. An academic from a young age, his first major discovery was the fossil remains of an ichthyosaurus in St Leonard's Forest.

He was a somewhat controversial character, drawing some criticism from his fellow Quakers for keeping a pack of hunting dogs at one of his large ancestral properties, and also from the local Tory party, who, at one election, burnt an effigy of him in the Carfax (he being a member of the opposing Liberal Party). As a side note, this appears to have been somewhat of a tradition at the time, since an effigy of the political activist and revolutionary, Thomas Paine, was also burned in the Carfax in 1792, and an effigy of the Shipley parish clerk was burnt outside his own front door for having spoken in favour of Paine.

His most famous discovery was perhaps the Great Horsham Iguanodon fossil, uncovered during the construction of St Mark's Church in 1840. Bax Holmes amassed a large collection of fossils (some of which are now on display at Horsham Museum). He was buried at the Friends Meeting House in Worthing Road in 1887.

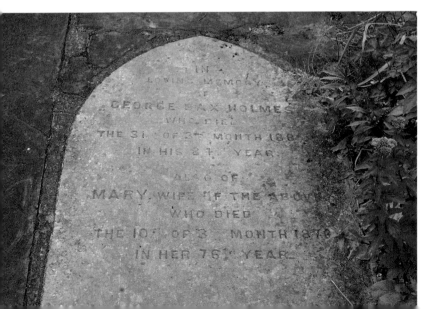

Bax Holmes' grave at the Friends Meeting House, Worthing Road.

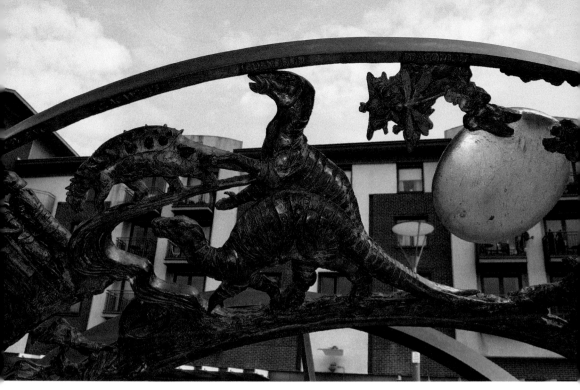

The Horshamosaurus (left) and iguanodon (right) on the sundial sculpture.

Further iguanodon fossils were uncovered at the former Southwater brickworks in November 1940. Southwater was also where other fossils were uncovered in 1925 and 1928, some of which are now on display at Beeson House.

Then, in 1985, a number of fossils were unearthed at the Rudgwick brickworks that were initially thought to have been more iguanodon remains, but were later discovered to be not only from a different species but were also unique, and the animal was officially named *Polacanthus rudgwickensis*. Further research in 2015 revealed the remains were actually from a different genus than previously believed, and the new species of *Horshamosaurus rudgwickensis* was named.

Blitz and Bombs

Horsham witnessed more than its fair share of wartime incidents. Between September 1940 and May 1945, seven civilians were killed and a further twenty-nine people wounded. At least sixty-four high-explosive bombs were dropped, as well as upwards of 100 incendiary and phosphorus bombs. There was one recorded case of aerial machine-gunning, and eight aircraft were shot down or crashed. Furthermore, three V-1 flying bombs were brought down in the area, though none actually fell on the built-up area of the town. There is not enough space to provide a full account of each and every incident that occurred, but some of the more notable ones are outlined below.

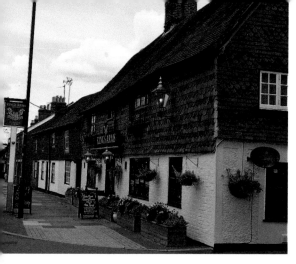

The Bishopric, attacked in 1942, and site of a public shelter.

On 7 October 1940, two high-explosive bombs fell on the Worthing Road railway crossing. A train was wrecked and the line blocked, but amazingly no casualties were sustained. At Farthings Farm (now the Farthings Walk area), eleven high-explosive bombs were dropped on 21 November 1940, though the only damage was to electricity cables, fences and windows. On 16 December 1942, it was reported that a German plane machine-gunned the Bishopric, though no damage or casualties were sustained. Excitement came to the Girl's High School (now Tanbridge House) on Worthing Road when they reported an incendiary bomb had hit the school and started a small fire. However, the next day it was discovered that it was in fact a cannon shell from a fighter rather than a bomb. A serious raid occurred on 10 February 1943, when four high-explosive bombs were dropped on the Wimblehurst Road and Richmond Road area. Two of the bombs scored direct hits on Orwell Lodge, the third on Red Tiles (both properties were destroyed), and the fourth fell in the garden of No. 12 Wimblehurst Road. Heavy damage was also caused to Craven Lodge, Nos 31a and 31b North Parade and to Sussex Lodge; a further seventeen houses were badly damaged and forty-nine slightly damaged. Somehow, no one was killed, though eight adults and two children were injured. All appear to have recovered from their injuries. However, the single worst air raid of the entire war was on 29 November 1940, when two high-explosive bombs were dropped on Orchard Road. Six houses were completely destroyed, eight more were later demolished and a further 110 houses were damaged in lesser degrees. Six people were killed (including three children – the youngest aged just six) at Nos 9, 10, 12 and 16 Orchard Road, and another seventeen people (including two children) were injured. Two of the fatalities were members of the local Home Guard, and nine-year-old Joan Elizabeth Hunt died later that day at Horsham Hospital. It would appear that most of the child victims were evacuees from London.

Broadbridge Heath did not escape undamaged either. On 20 November, a German plane crashed south of the Post Office (now No. 34 Old Guildford Road), seriously damaging two houses and causing slight damage to a further 265 houses and shops. The pilot survived and was taken into custody.

It was on 29 June 1944 that the first V-1 arrived and was shot down by fighters before crashing and exploding just north of Christ's Hospital School. It damaged some of

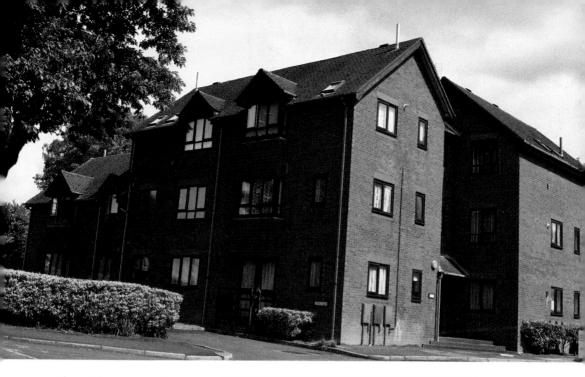

Above: The post-war Sussex Lodge, rebuilt after being bombed.

Right: The north end of Orchard Road, scene of Horsham's worst air raid.

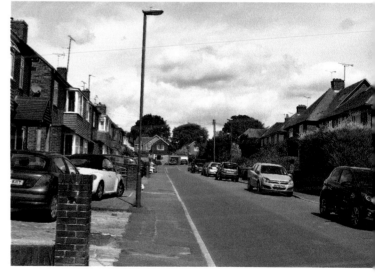

the nearby buildings and injured one person. It was also recorded that the explosion damaged 'numerous windows ... in buildings including shop windows in The Bishopric + West Street' over 1.5 miles away! The second V-1 fell on 21 July, exploding at Chesworth Farm, just west of Kerves Lane, though the only casualties were some broken windows and 'considerable damage to [a] field of wheat'. The third and final V-1 exploded in St Leonard's Forest at Highlands Farm on 29 July. Fortunately, there was only one slight casualty and only minor damage to five properties (including St Leonard's Forest House, which had the windows and doors blown in). One of the last, but more intriguing, incidents came on 15 August 1944, when a French incendiary bomb fell near Nuthurst, though it failed to ignite and was taken for safe keeping at the Barttelot Road police station. Presumably, this had been captured during the invasion of France before being dropped on Horsham a few years later.

Many bombs dropped on Horsham failed to explode, and it was the duty of the bomb disposal units, whose headquarters were at Broadbridge Heath (on the present site of the Tesco supermarket and leisure centre), to render them safe. The men remained at Broadbridge Heath until the early 1960s, dealing with the thousands of bombs that were still being uncovered across the UK. During the present redevelopment works on the site, a 1,000-lb bomb was discovered, though thankfully it had been defused decades ago and the explosive removed. It is now on display at the Wings Museum near Balcombe.

The civilian population wasn't entirely vulnerable to attack, however. A number of air-raid shelters were provided in the town, including one for 150 people adjacent to the old Star public house on Crawley Road (close to the site of the present Star), another for 200 people adjacent to the old Capitol Theatre (now demolished and on the site of Swan Walk shopping centre), a long, narrow shelter for 150 people in East Street that stretched across what is now the junction of the A281 with East Street. A 100-person shelter was located in the Bishopric outside the Green Dragon pub (now the King's Arms), a small fifty-person shelter in South Street at what are now disabled parking bays beside the Comodor Restaurant, another one in the Carfax approximately where the *West Sussex County Times* sculpture is, and another fifty-person shelter on the island at the northern end of The Causeway.

An air-raid shelter once stood at the end of The Causeway.

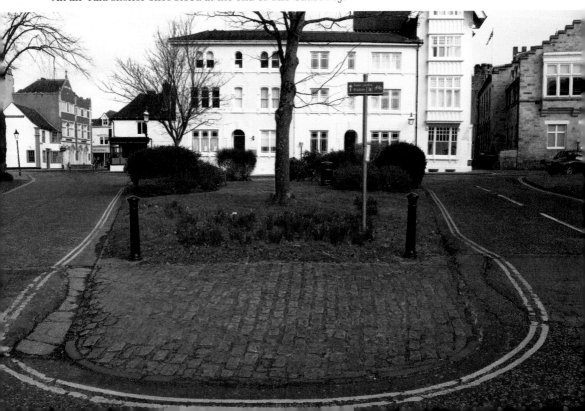

C

Church of St Mary the Virgin

As with most towns and villages, the church is the oldest surviving building in Horsham, dating back to 1247, although traces of the earlier Norman church can still be found in the tower and the west door (which also has much carved

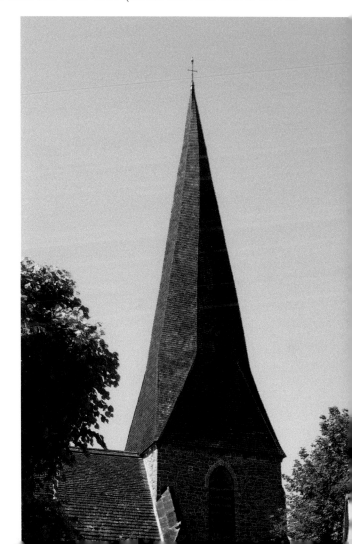

The twisted spire of St Mary's Church.

graffiti of various ages). One unique feature is the tall, shingled spire, which has a noticeable twist as it extends upwards. Whether this was an intentional design is not known. The tower also features a corbel table immediately under the eaves, comprising numerous human and animal faces in various poses. Inside, there are some interesting features, including a stuffed owl hidden high up in the rafters, some tombs of great antiquity and the colours of the Experimental Corps of Riflemen. The latter was formed in Horsham in 1800 at Barrack Field (now the cricket field) and was later renamed the 95th Rifles – one of the most famous and highly decorated regiments of the British Army. To the east of the church is the area known as Normandy, at the westernmost end of which, at what is now a private car park beside the former almshouses, once stood the Priest House. It was here that an ancient well – the Normandy Well – was located. It appears to be one of the few holy wells that was retained for use by the Church until sometime in the twentieth century, with the water from the well used in baptisms.

The church also has a significant 21.2° orientation to the south of true east. There are many theories as to why medieval churches are not always on an east–west alignment, including orientation to the sunrise on a particular saint's day. Whether intentional or not, it is interesting to note that St Mary's Church is almost in alignment with the Church of the Holy Sepulchre in Jerusalem – just 1.5° off, which over a distance of 2,240 miles is quite impressive.

St Mary the Virgin Church.

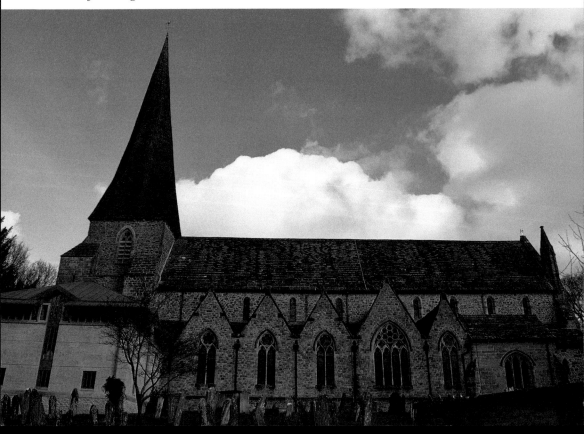

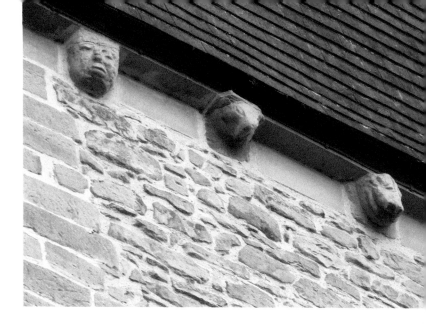

Some of the corbel table carvings on the spire.

Cruel Crimes and Unusual Punishments

As an assize town for much of its history, Horsham was no stranger to dealing with horrific crimes and meting out punishments (often severe) for the slightest offence. It is somewhat surprising from a modern perspective that a small debt had the potential to see a person locked away for life.

Smuggling was a particular problem for Horsham, and although there are more tales than there is room to write, there are a few cases of particular interest. The first was in July 1714 when two French sailors, Francis Freques and John Coqvele, who had robbed other ships in the Channel and then assaulted and robbed the customs officer at Seaford, were apprehended at Littlehampton when their treasure ship ran aground. They were taken to Horsham for trial, but the jury acquitted the men since the crimes were committed on the high seas and the customs officer had agreed to cease his prosecution on condition that all his belongings were returned. On 24 September 1745, James Roe and William Winter (alias Black Sam) were imprisoned at Horsham. However, it was not always the smugglers who were in trouble. On 11 March 1774, a soldier was sent to Horsham Gaol after being found guilty of the wilful murder of a smuggler he was apprehending. Another surprising case took place in August 1792, when the smuggler John Pettit (alias Jigg) was acquitted at Horsham for the crime of stealing his own horse!

Being a military garrison town with its own barracks, it was not uncommon for soldiers to find themselves in the dock. In 1786, Thomas Watts and James Wilders were arrested and tried at Horsham for assaulting and robbing a Mr Hart near Lewes. During the trial, the men admitted to three more robberies. Watts also informed on a third soldier, John Ross, for two of the above crimes, who was later arrested and brought to Horsham.

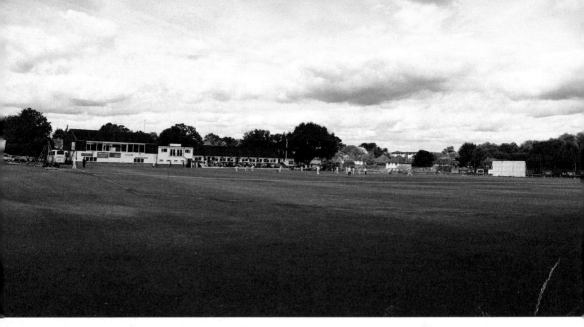

Barrack Field, where the barracks once existed.

In 1795, thirteen Oxfordshire militiamen were convicted by court martial at Brighton for rioting and stealing. Two of them, James Sykes and William Sansom, were taken to Horsham and were publically hanged on 13 June, with two executioners from the Old Bailey being brought down especially, and several representatives of the county authorities in attendance to witness the event. Despite 'expert' executioners being employed, Sansom's death was especially painful after his hair was caught in the noose.

This very public and brutal warning did not stop local soldiers from committing crimes in the town. On 9 July 1798, twelve soldiers from Horsham Barracks were charged with highway robbery for stopping a Mr Sadler near Pix Hill and robbing him of four cheeses, a tub of butter and a bag of oatmeal. This was followed on 25 February 1801 by two soldiers of the 16th Dragoons being sent to Horsham Gaol for breaking and entering several houses across Sussex.

When researching historic crimes, another common term found is that of the so-called 'unnatural offences'. This was a cover-all term used for a number of crimes that included sodomy, bestiality, paedophilia and incest. Several cases of 'unnatural crimes' were uncovered for Horsham. One was on 23 August 1892 when a young lad was charged with an unnatural offence with a horse in the stable of the Swan Inn in West Street (now the site of Jones shoe shop). He was found guilty, but the jury asked for leniency and he was duly sentenced to three months' imprisonment and hard labour for this otherwise capital offence. The issue of leniency is somewhat called into question, however, considering that at the same assizes, Edward Bartlett, who pleaded guilty to indecently assaulting ten-year-old Ellen Gumm on 17 August 1892, was sentenced to just three months' imprisonment, reduced to one month for time already served awaiting trial. Another took place on 8 October 1810 when a seventy-seven-year-old man was charged with an 'unnatural crime' with a boy aged

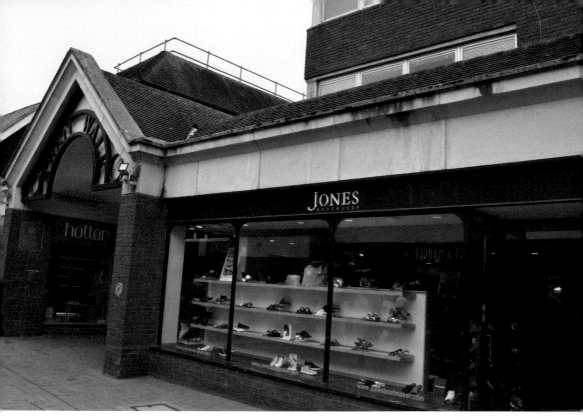
Jones Bootmakers is on the site of the former Swan Inn.

fourteen, whom he had seduced into committing the act. The man had been known to have frequented the river banks at Ifield for several months prior to his arrest. Fast forward almost a century, and James Robinson, another elderly man, was in court at Horsham on 16 August 1909 for attempting to commit an 'unnatural offence' at Chennell's Brook with a group of young boys he had been watching paddling. He denied his crime at first, but at his trial he admitted it, saying he had no remorse for his crime.

In one particularly shocking case, on 11 June 1774, the bodies of two babies were found at the house of a Mrs Smith at Shipley, both showing signs of extremely violent deaths. A young girl had been shown the bodies by Mrs Smith's sons and, having told the maid what she saw, the maid went to investigate and found the bodies for herself. She carefully put them in a basket and took them to the coroner in Horsham, who ruled that Mrs Smith was probably innocent of the crime since she stated that she had found the bodies when the family moved in two years previously, despite the fact that at least one of the babies had been dead for no longer than a year. A journalist reporting on the story was not quite as convinced as to Mrs Smith's innocence.

As the county gaol, Horsham was also the scene of almost all of the executions in Sussex up until 1844. Between 1735 and 1844, there were 129 recorded executions in the town. The most number of people executed at once was five, on 29 July 1606, when Thomas Welch, Simon Ayers, Robert Planer, Marget Squire and Elisabeth Waterman were all hanged. All the executions at Horsham were public affairs,

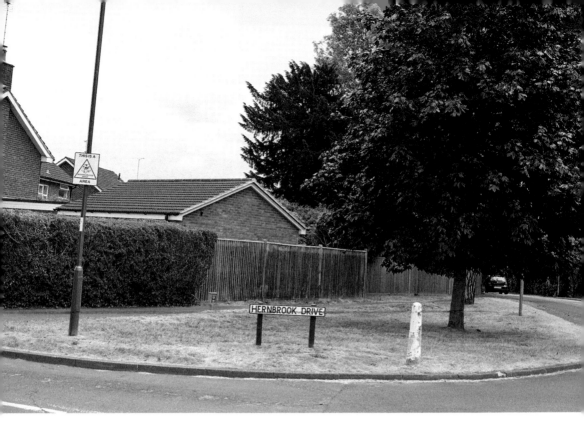

The Hanging Plat was where these houses off Hernbrook Drive are today.

and so common were they that they became known as the Horsham Hang Fair, with large crowds often gathering and school children given the day off to observe the events. There is not enough space in this book to relate every case, so a few particularly notable cases have been picked out. Until 1822, all executions took place on Horsham Common – once a large expanse of land to the north and east of the town centre. The original location of the executions prior to August 1779 was along Kings Road, approximately in the grounds of Garden Cottage (almost opposite the junction with Kingslea). From then, hangings took place on a plot of land once known as the Hanging Plat, opposite the junction of Kerves Lane with Brighton Road until 1822, when executions took place on gallows outside the entrance to the East Street gaol. Throughout most of the time that Horsham was the place of execution, the morbid custom of stroking the dead man's hand across the necks of women and girls with skin complaints was carried out, with the last specifically reported instance being in the early 1820s.

On 22 August 1835, nineteen-year-old James Sparsholt was hanged at the gaol for sodomy. He was not the youngest to be hanged, since a thirteen-year-old boy is known to have suffered the noose at Horsham. The youngest female executed was eighteen-year-old Elizabeth Lavender, who was hanged on 22 July 1799 for the murder of her newborn child. The child had been fathered by Elizabeth's own father (it's not clear if she was forced into the act) and she killed the baby in an act of desperation when her father tried to get her to pretend the child belonged to another man. Her father was sent to gaol. On 26 July 1788, William Still was hanged for horse stealing. He had a particularly slow and agonising death when the executioner turned up extremely drunk and did not carry out the hanging properly.

The most notorious criminal executed was John Holloway for the violent murder of his wife. He was hanged on 16 December 1831, but it was events at his trial and imprisonment that brought him particular notoriety. At his court appearance, he lashed out at a ten-year-old boy in the crowd, hitting him square between the eyes. Then, while in Horsham Gaol, he formed a gang with other prisoners and they conspired to murder the gaolers and governor and then make their escape, but the plot was revealed by another prisoner. After his execution, Holloway was taken to Brighton for public dissection. Richard Grazemark is the earliest recorded male dissected at Horsham when he was executed on Horsham Common in 1790 for murdering his daughter, with whom he had fathered several children. She had secretly married another local man, and after several failed attempts to kill the husband, Grazemark killed his daughter so that no other man could be with her.

Daniel Hartford was the last person executed on Horsham Common on 19 August 1820 (his crime: horse stealing), whereas Henry Durrant and James Tilley became the first to be executed at the gaol on 24 August 1822 for burglary. The final execution at Horsham was that of John Lawrence on 6 April 1844, who had murdered the chief constable of Brighton with a poker during questioning for a carpet theft. About three thousand people turned out to watch the event in East Street.

The modern building bears a striking resemblance to the fourth gaol.

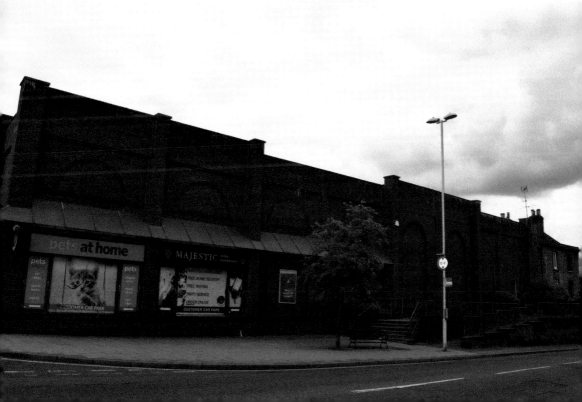

Not all executions were of guilty persons, however. Nineteen-year-old George Wren pleaded innocence all the way to the end when he was hanged on 5 January 1833 for firing a haystack. The actual perpetrator admitted to the crime many years later.

Hanging was not the only method employed for execution at Horsham. Anne Whale was burned at the stake at Broadbridge Heath on 14 August 1752 for the murder of her husband; her accomplice, Sarah Pledge, was hanged. Pledge became the first female in the country to be publically dissected after it became law in 1751. On 8 August 1776, seventy-three-year-old Anne Cruttenden was tied to a hurdle and dragged to Horsham Common where she was burned at the stake for murdering her husband; she was the last person in Sussex to suffer such a fate. It was only forty years earlier that John Weekes had a particularly long and painful death when he became the last person in the country to be pressed to death. The event happened in the gaol yard (and not on Gaol Green as many sources like to surmise – no executions ever took place in the Carfax) on 11 August 1735 for failing to enter a plea on a charge of murder. The theory is that by refusing to enter a plea, his property would not have been seized from his family after his death. It took the 224-lb weight of the executioner, on top of the 400 lbs already added, to finally squeeze the last of the life out of him. The scene was said to have been so horrific that many spectators were shaken for a long time afterwards.

There was at least one recorded time that a woman acted as the hangman at Horsham, in 1758, when the actual executioner was unable to carry out the task himself, and his wife stepped in to take over. The names of the prisoners were not recorded, but other records state the only executions for 1758 were those of John Noyse and John Weak on 27 July for murder.

Earlier executions are occasionally recorded at Horsham, the earliest being in the fourteenth century. Another, John Burden, was executed on Horsham Common on 29 April 1515 for deer poaching. The church register, dating to 1540, also provides insight into other early crimes. On 15 June 1541, Rycherd Sowton was hanged for forging coins at Nuthurst. On 10 October 1608, Laurence Lambert and Richard Harris were executed on Horsham Common, as was John Davis on 18 July 1614, and William Fludd and William Osborne on 25 March 1626. One of the earliest recorded Jewish serial killers was also executed when Jacob Harris was hanged on Horsham Common in 1734 for killing three people at Ditchling. His body was sent to Ditchling afterwards to be displayed in chains at the scene of his crimes.

Horsham also had other methods of punishment for lesser crimes. Replica stocks and a whipping post stand in the Carfax today (the real whipping post being on display at Horsham Museum). However, before the stocks and whipping post were introduced, it appears that Horsham had a pillory, since Thomas Brice was sentenced to stand in it on 9 July 1785. After this date, the now familiar stocks and post were used, though the original ones were clearly a much feared sight and did not last long when, on 18 July 1791, William Sherlock was convicted for being a 'profane swearer' and for destroying the stocks and whipping post. New ones were made up and put

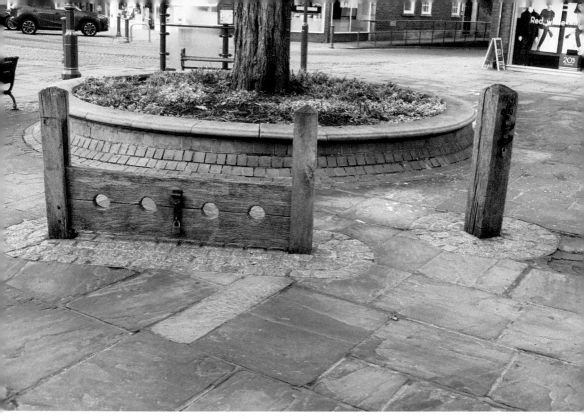

Replica stocks and whipping post in the Carfax.

back into use. These stocks were rediscovered in 1859 in the fire engine house near Hewells Manor, and were burned on a bonfire at the town's 5 November celebrations that year. On 12 July 1785, Richard Denyer was convicted of stealing 16 feet of oak planks and was sentenced to three months' imprisonment and then to 'be severely whipped at the cart's tail round the market-place' (this meant he was stripped semi-naked, hands tied to the back of a cart and forced to walk around the Carfax and Market Square while being whipped 'until his body be bloody'). The last instance of flogging in relation to Horsham took place in 1930, when John Jones was sentenced to twenty lashes (in addition to imprisonment and hard labour) at Lewes for assaulting and robbing a taxicab driver at Lower Beeding on 17 August 1929, having come to Horsham in search of a judge who had sentenced him for a previous crime.

There is no recorded case of ducking at Horsham, but there is one for nearby Billingshurst when, on 20 January 1747, a man who was known to have abused his long-suffering wife and maid was driven out of his house by the women of the village (with the assistance of some men) and, as soon as he appeared at the door, was quickly wrapped in a blanket and carried to the village pond where he was ducked several times in front of a crowd of several hundred people. He was only released once he had promised to never lay a finger on his wife again.

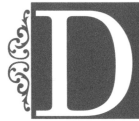

Dead and Buried in Horsham

Denne Road Cemetery closed about a century ago and was superseded by Hills Cemetery on the other side of the town. It is now known for the Peace Garden that still hosts an annual service to commemorate the bombing of Hiroshima and Nagasaki in 1945. Found at Denne Road is a memorial to Horsham's youngest war casualty, fifteen-year-old

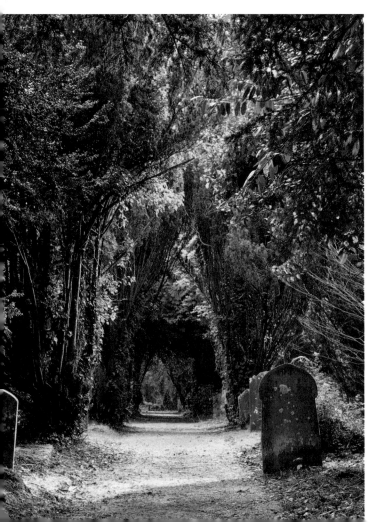

The Denne Road Cemetery, now a wildlife haven.

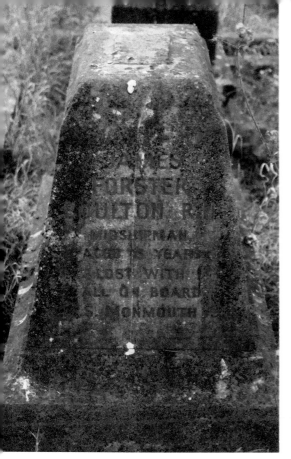

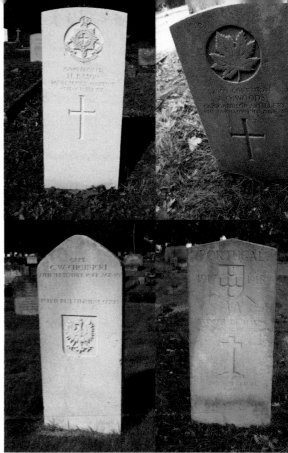

Above left: James Forster Boulton memorial, Denne Road.

Above right: The four nations buried at Hills today.

James Forster Boulton, who was killed aboard HMS *Monmouth* on 1 November 1914. Hills at one time had military graves to servicemen of five different nations (British, Canadian, Portuguese, Polish and German), but in the 1950s all German airmen were removed to Cannock Chase. Two of them had been buried together in September 1940. The first, unnamed, had a single red rose placed on his coffin, while the coffin of Ober Lieutnant Paul Waechter was inscribed with a small swastika. During the burial of another German airman at Hills, an air raid occurred in the middle of the ceremony.

At St Mary's Church is a grave that is aligned north–south. This is the resting place of Helena Bennett (originally Noor Begum), a Persian princess who converted to Catholicism and came to England in 1797 after being abandoned by her husband, and adopted the name Helena Bennett. She first lived at Colgate Lodge before moving to Horsham to live at Rangers Lodge in St Leonard's Forest. It was at Rangers Lodge that Helena was the victim of several crimes. The first was in April 1840 when a quantity of jewellery, a writing desk and other items were taken by masked men before being burnt in an open field a short distance away. Secondly, in October 1844, John Hoar was convicted of stealing four geese from her. Lastly, in October 1846, William Newman was in court for having threatened to physically attack her. She died in January 1854

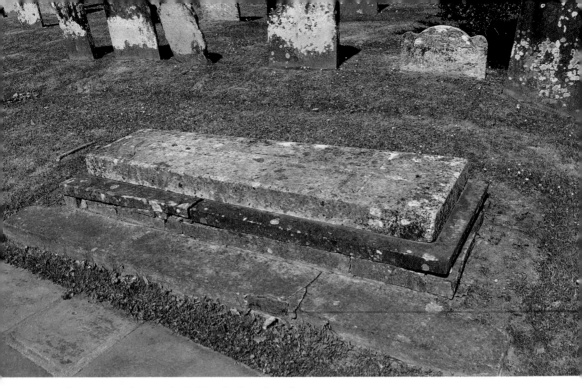

Helena Bennett's grave in St Mary's churchyard.

and by this time she had moved to a house in North Street, where her possessions were auctioned off on 31 January and 1 February 1854. A short distance away, on the opposite side of the footpath is another, ornately carved, headstone that faces north–south.

In April 1797, it was reported that husband and wife Joseph and Mary Gatford both died on the same day within two hours of each other, and that both had also been born on the same day seventy-eight years earlier. Two years later, Elizabeth Gatford requested a highly unusual ceremony to be provided for her burial. This was to consist of being placed inside a lead coffin, in turn inserted in a stone coffin, and to remain unburied for twenty-one days. This necessitated for the coffin to be filled with £20 worth of wine to preserve the body. Then, when it came time for burial, she insisted that it must take place after 10.00 p.m. Her wishes were duly granted and at midnight on the day of her burial, she was interred in a vault under the Worthing Road Baptist Chapel.

At first appearance, an 1827 edition of the *Brighton Guardian* relates a burial of a true giant at Horsham by the name of Mr W. Agate. It is stated that he weighed 126 stone and was buried in a coffin measuring 17 feet long, 13 feet wide and over 12 feet deep. These unbelievable proportions were later found to be a hoax, with the notice having been intercepted in the post and someone adding a '1' before each of the original numbers (making him 26 stone rather than 126 stone, etc).

A particularly sad case was that of Ursley Mascall who suddenly died when journeying through Horsham on the way to a wedding and was buried at St Mary's churchyard on 1 August 1612. Another unfortunate end came for Elizabeth Stroode, who was buried at St Mary's churchyard on 19 August 1615 after she was killed standing under the belfry door when the steeple was hit by lightning.

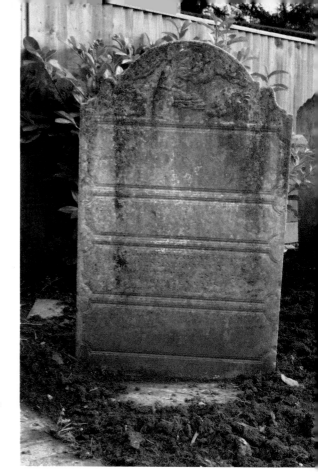

Right: Another north–south aligned grave in the churchyard.

Below: Worthing Road Baptist Chapel, scene of an unusual burial.

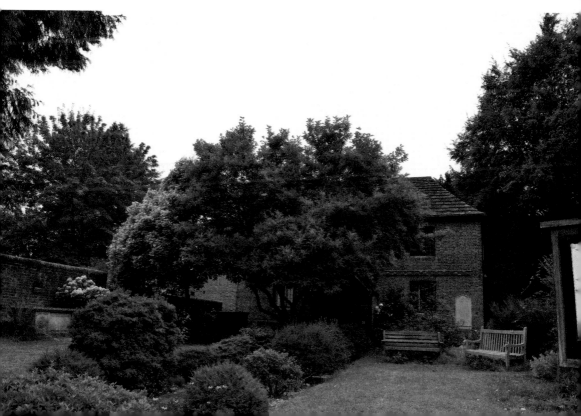

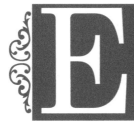

Education: A Blue Coat School

Although not opened until the start of the twentieth century, the origins of Christ's Hospital School at Horsham date back at least a decade beforehand. At first there were objections to the plans to relocate the school, with one of the main points being that the site was 'unhealthy'. In a strange twist, this objection by locals resulted in the town actually embracing the school, since it was a concern that the town would have been tarnished as dirty if the plans were dropped. A party of forty officials visited the site in June 1896 to determine its suitability, staying at Warnham Lodge as the guests of Mr Harben (who later became a leading male supporter of women's suffrage).

An ornate gatehouse at Christ's Hospital School.

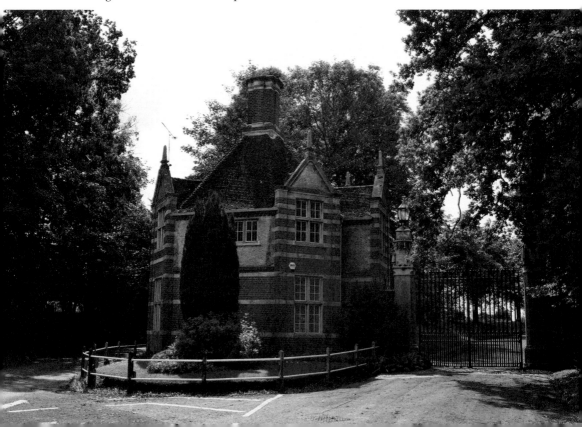

On 23 October 1897, the Prince of Wales (later King Edward VII) laid the foundation stone in a full Masonic ritual using a trowel that his forebear had used in laying the foundation stone of the Great Hall at the original site of Christ's Hospital School in London in 1825. Original parts of the old buildings were carefully dismantled and rebuilt at the Horsham site, including one of the ancient gateways, statues and an eighty-seven-foot-long painting that once hung in the old hall.

During the construction works, five casualties were caused. The first was fatal and occurred on 1 May 1899 when Seth Evans fell from some scaffolding and was found on the ground unconscious. He later died from a fractured skull and ruptured frontal lobe. The second occurred on 24 June 1901 when four workmen were trapped under rubble when the archway and ceiling in a corridor leading to the classrooms collapsed on top of them. Remarkably, they suffered only minor injuries. In addition, in 1902 there was a smallpox outbreak at the site, though this thankfully appears to have been an isolated incident that did not spread.

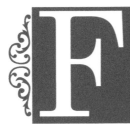

Fascism: A Black(shirt) Stain on Horsham

Horsham, today, is very much considered a Conservative stronghold. You would need to go as far back as the 1876 by-election to find the last time that the town returned a non-Conservative MP. However, for some six years between 1934 and 1940 a very different kind of politics swept through Horsham: the blackshirts of Oswald Mosley's British Union of Fascists.

Horsham had not just one, but two bases for the BUF. The first was at No. 46a West Street (part of what is now Joules), which was set up in August 1934 when it shared the building with the Christian Science Society Reading Room, and is last mentioned

Formerly 46a West Street, now Joules, site of the first BUF headquarters.

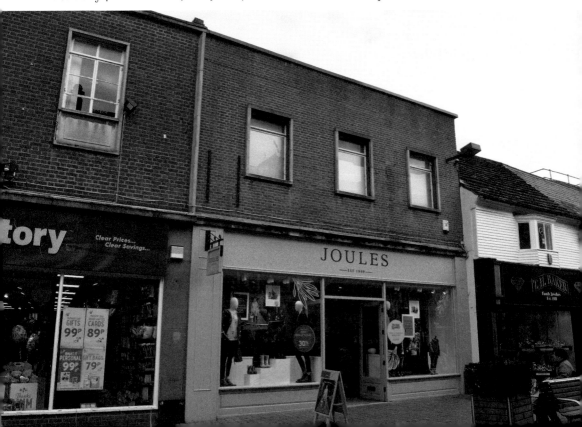

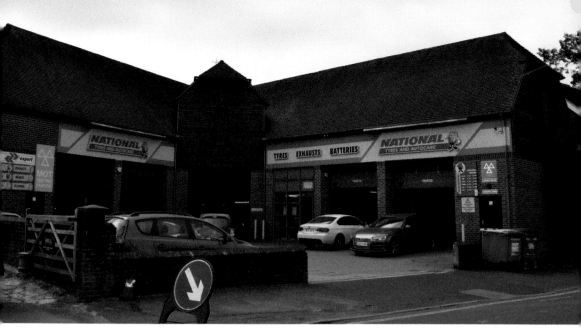

The second BUF headquarters is believed to have adjoined No. 11 Denne Road.

in October 1935. The second base, which seems to have been established in 1936, was in Denne Road in a small, now demolished, building adjacent to No. 11 Denne Road, where National Tyres and Autocare now stands. The outside of the building was festooned with fascist posters and prominently displayed the BUF thunderbolt.

The first fascist event in Horsham was on 12 January 1934, when the BUF held a public meeting; the Horsham branch having been formed in late December 1933 by F. A. C. Boothby and Arnold Lancaster, who had gained permission from the council to hire the town hall for future meetings. A second public meeting, this time hosted by the infamous William Joyce (later better known as Lord Haw-Haw), occurred on 23 June 1934 at the Drill Hall in Denne Road. Just a few days earlier, on 19 June, a fleet of blackshirt vans descended on the town as part of a national propaganda tour of the rural towns. This was followed by a blackshirt dance at Rusper Village Hall on 16 August. This dance appears to have been, for a short time at least, a fairly regular event, since another took place there five months later when Stan Redford, the church organist, provided the music. William Joyce returned to Horsham on 17 August 1934 with another large public meeting, this time at the town hall. Also present at this meeting was Captain Charles Bentinck-Budd, who became the UK's first fascist councillor to take office when elected to West Sussex County Council and Worthing Borough Council in 1933. The final event of 1934 was an open-air meeting in the Carfax on 8 December, hosted by J. L. Crosland, the son of the vicar of Rustington.

The following year saw more fascist events in Horsham, beginning with another blackshirt dance at Rusper Village Hall on 10 January. The local branch also began sales drives of their newspapers in the Carfax in August. More than 1,500 copies of *Blackshirt* had been sold to Horsham residents during the previous year, principally by May Chateris Goodman (a chiropodist and masseuse living at No. 70 Hurst Road), and if these figures are true, then this would represent around 10 per cent of the town's population at the time. It was in 1935 that the Horsham branch also formed a cricket team captained by E. Lumsden. However, not all was well within the Sussex BUF in 1935, since Bentinck-Budd was in court at the Old Town Hall for allegedly threatening to shoot Harry Jones, the officer-in-charge of the Horsham branch, who had known the whereabouts of Bentinck-Budd's wife and child (who had deserted him in January). The court dismissed the charges and the defendant was free to go.

The following year, 1936, appears to have been the pinnacle of fascist activity in Horsham, but was also when opposition first began to materialise. The first event of that year, on 11 January, was a sales drive and open-air meeting in the Carfax. This marked the start of weekly fascist gatherings in the Carfax on Saturdays, and sometimes attracted high-profile visitors from the BUF. It would appear that the local authorities had seen enough by this stage and the police broke up one gathering on 15 May that had become rowdy. Albert Edward Laker, of No. 35 Roffey Road, was arrested for being drunk and disorderly after he had offered to fight the blackshirts. This did not stop the BUF from gaining momentum, however, and at the end of May, further public meetings had taken place in the Carfax. On 7 May, John Beckett, the editor of *Action*, another BUF newspaper, addressed a meeting at the town hall. It was also at the end of May that the Horsham branch had formed a children's section that already had seven school-age children as members. In early June, this had grown to fourteen children. The police implemented a complete ban on public meetings

The Carfax was where many fascist meetings were held.

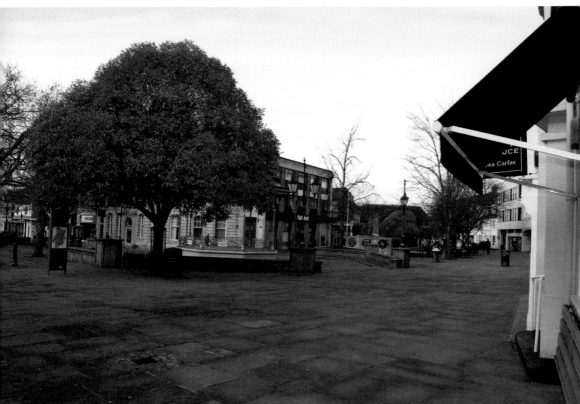

in the Carfax from June 1936, although the BUF attempted to defy the ban on the 17th, but were prevented from doing so. This seems to have put a temporary halt to activities, although on 14 August District Officer Warren John Willard was in court for having thrown leaflets advertising a fascist meeting out of a moving vehicle as it drove along West Street. In early November, the weekly gatherings moved to Market Square. It was at one of the November meetings that it was announced that Jorian Jenks was to stand as the BUF candidate for Horsham at the next election. In addition, on 26 November another meeting at the town hall was held for the local farmers to be introduced to Jenks, and another was held there on 3 December when J. A. MacNab, of national headquarters, was the chief speaker.

The weekly meetings seem to have ended in late December, but resumed in February 1937. By now it was claimed that seven newsagents around the town advertised fascist newspapers, and in late April, Clifford Donald Underhill, an insurance broker at No. 42 Bedford Road, offered to cover all members of the Horsham BUF.

In the last few years of the BUF's existence, activity in Horsham tailed off. Posters were displayed around the town in April 1938, and in August H. J. Duffield newsagents, at 40 East Street, began to stock *Action*. Monthly meetings (as opposed to the weekly ones of previous years) commenced again on 3 September 1938. This meeting ended up in heated debates with the crowd when the final speaker, Mr Swift, took the stage and refused to confirm or deny whether the BUF were supportive of Hitler's invasion of

Formerly Duffield's, No. 40 East Street is still a newsagents today.

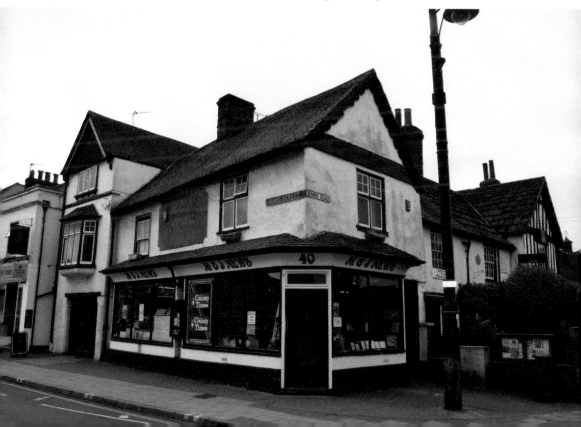

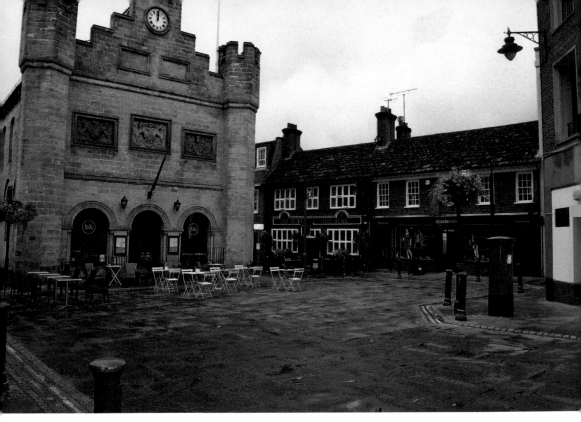

Market Square, scene of several rowdy fascist meetings.

Czechoslovakia. The meeting held on 28 October in Market Square had to be broken up by police when most of the 1,000 people attending were anti-fascist and began heckling the speaker, Mr Rossiter. When John Blair took the stage he threatened the opponents in the crowd and the audience began to throw lit cigarettes and fireworks at him; the meeting eventually turned into a brawl between the blackshirts and the townspeople. The police intervened and escorted the blackshirts along East Street and to the BUF headquarters in Denne Road, followed by a large part of the crowd who had to be prevented from entering.

The first event of 1939 came on 7 January when C. H. Luckin, the editor of *Action*, and John Blair, Worthing District Leader, addressed a small gathering in Market Square, with Luckin principally spouting anti-Semitic policies. Extra police had been drafted in for the event, but were not needed. However, the biggest event came just seven months before war broke out, on 22 February 1939. It was on this date that Oswald Mosley himself hosted a public meeting at the Drill Hall. Reports vary as to attendance, with figures varying between 500 and 1,000 people. This is the only recorded visit by Mosley to Horsham; however, his grandfather (also named Sir Oswald) lived at Abingworth in nearby Thakeham and his great uncle, Ernald Mosley, lived at Monks Gate House (a few miles outside of town) until his death in 1933 when a memorial service was held at Lower Beeding Church. The house then passed to Oswald's brother, John. It appears from his autobiography that Mosley had spent time at both places in his pre-fascist days and was familiar with Monks Gate House during the time of the BUF.

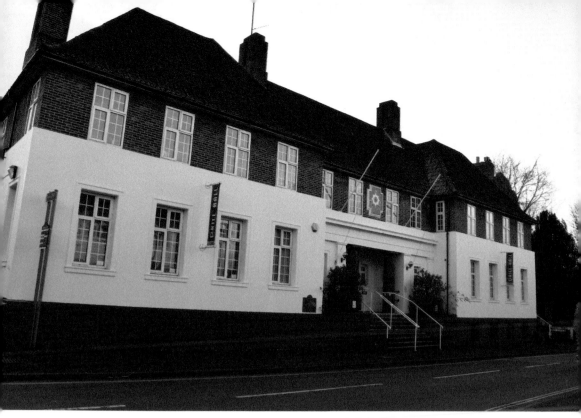

The Drill Hall was host to both William Joyce and Oswald Mosley.

With war breaking out, the Horsham BUF were still active in 1940. On 21 March, the hard-line fascist Alexander Raven Thomson held a public meeting on BUF policy and the war at the W.I. Market Hall in the Carfax (the site now being Crew Clothing Company). The final BUF event came on 18 May when a lone female attempted to address a hostile crowd of 500 people in Market Square for an hour before finally being cut off by the crowd loudly singing 'There'll always be an England'.

It was also in 1940 that the government passed Defence Regulation 18B, which led to the internment without trial of suspected Nazi sympathisers and the banning of the BUF in May of that year. Several people were being monitored by MI5, including Major Eric Shufflebotham, of No. 60 Guildford Road, manager of the National Provincial Bank (now the Anchor Hotel). Shufflebotham had also been the president of Horsham Chamber of Trade, treasurer of Horsham Swimming Club and also the chief air-raid warden until he went to Exeter in June 1941. Furthermore, at least two Horsham residents were actually arrested and interned in detention camps in June 1940: Ronald Hasselgrave Greenfield (a bank clerk and the Horsham propaganda officer, of No. 9 West Parade) and Alfred Nightingale (a launderer and the Horsham unit leader, of No. 22 Hurst Road,); they were both released in January 1941. When news of Mosley's release from internment came in December 1943, the local Communist Party held a protest meeting at the W.I. Market Hall on 4 December, with the attendees (just twelve in number) agreeing to send a resolution to the town's MP to protest the release.

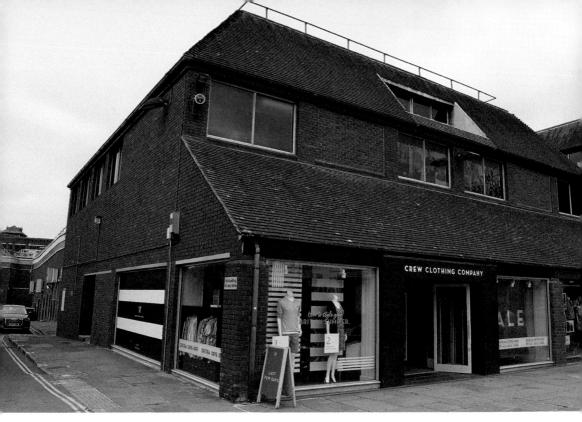

Crew Clothing Company stands on the site of the W.I. Market Hall.

The town's links with the far-right didn't end there, however. On 20 August 1949, a couple of eighteen-year-old members of the newly formed Union Movement attempted to host a meeting in Market Square, drawing an audience of one. They then moved to a nearby pub and again tried to broadcast their views to the customers, without success. National Front candidates were fielded for the constituency in 1974 and 1979, and the BNP stood candidates in local elections in Horsham between 2006 and 2009. In 2008 there was some local angst when the media reported that the local BNP were invited to parade and lay a wreath at the Horsham Remembrance Day ceremony, resulting in organisers denying that any group had been invited to attend. More recently, there have been several reports of a fascist group attending events in the town between 2014 and 2017, most notably at a European Election meeting at the Drill Hall.

G

Gaols

Most sources state that Horsham has had three gaols in its history, though it seems that there have actually been four. The first (which is often omitted) dated to around 1514 when a religious institution somewhere in North Street (said to have been north of Tysmans House, now long since demolished, but probably somewhere in the region of Albion Way as it passes under the RSA building) was dissolved and the building converted for use as a gaol. The second gaol was at the junction of the Carfax and North Street. Some difference of opinion is expressed here too, since most sources state that the only surviving part of this gaol was the gaoler's house, which is now Crates Local

Horsham's first gaol may have been located here.

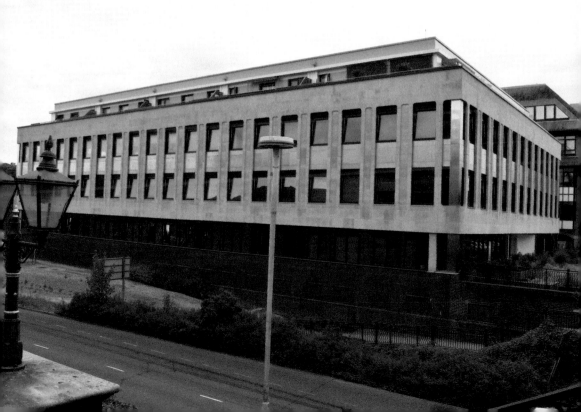

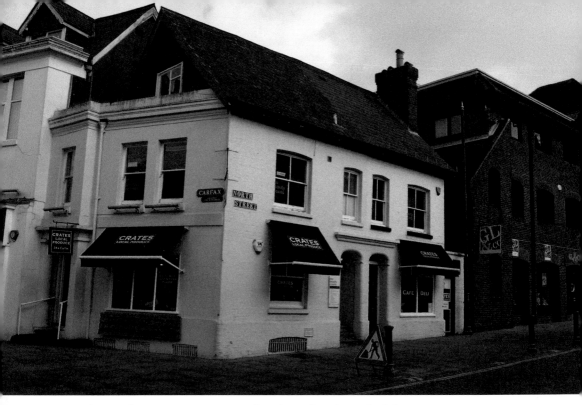

Depending on the source, Crates was either the gaol or the gaoler's house.

Produce shop, and that the gaol itself (demolished) was immediately to the north of this building. However, a map of 1792 has it the other way around – the gaol was at Crates and the gaoler's house was to the north. This latter fact is supported by William Albery's statement in *A Millennium of Facts* that the gaoler's house (as opposed to the gaol) was demolished in 1866, therefore placing Crates as the actual gaol building.

The third gaol, built around 1640, was just a short distance west of Crates. Although it was purposely built for the task, the conditions inside were horrendous. After John Howard's scandalous assessment of the facility in 1774 that branded the gaol as filthy and unsafe, too small for the number of prisoners, and highlighted the fact that prisoners were permanently detained in their cells with no chance of fresh air, plans were put forward for a fourth gaol built to modern standards. A plot of land was purchased in East Street, just beside the present railway bridge where Pets At Home and Majestic Wine are today. The prison, chapel, infirmary and gaoler's house were all completed by August 1779. This new gaol was the first in the country to have separate accommodation for debtors and felons, and to separate male and female prisoners. Previous gaols had put males and females together, which resulted in a number of prison marriages and the births of several children. This final gaol was demolished in 1844 and Petworth took over Horsham's 300-year-long role as the Sussex County Gaol.

There are several recorded instances of gaol breakers. One occurred in September 1762 when Richard Voller managed to escape justice. Another occurred in late 1773 when John Parker, a capital convict, escaped. Interestingly, a reward of four guineas was offered for Voller, but only two guineas for Parker.

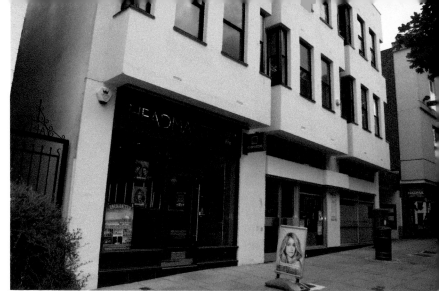

The town's third gaol once occupied this site in the Carfax.

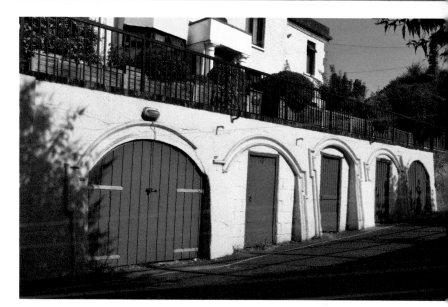

These cellars may once have been part of the fourth gaol.

During the seventeenth century, Quakers were persecuted severely in Sussex, and many found themselves locked up in Horsham Gaol, including such notable figures as Ambrose Rigge (who married his wife, Mary Luxford, in the gaol in 1664), George Fox, and William Penn (the founder of the Blue Idol at Coolham and of the State of Pennsylvania). With the unsanitary conditions of the gaol, many Quakers died and were buried at the Blue Idol Meeting House.

Two other notable prisoners were confined at Horsham. One was eighty-two-year-old Simon Southward, who died in the gaol in June 1810. He worked as a miller until 1766 when he assumed the identity of the Earl of Derby and gave up his work. The following year he was arrested and imprisoned for a small debt and ended up spending his remaining forty-three years, four months and eight days locked up in Horsham. He refused to respond to his gaolers or other prisoners unless they addressed him as 'my lord'. The second

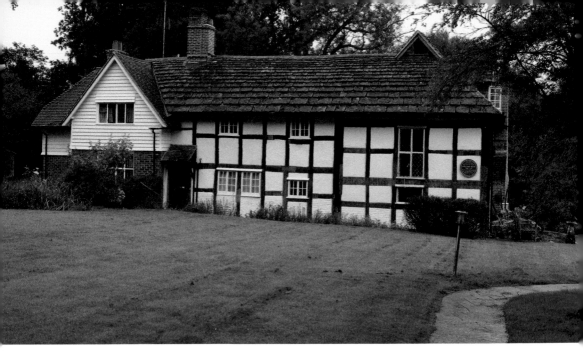

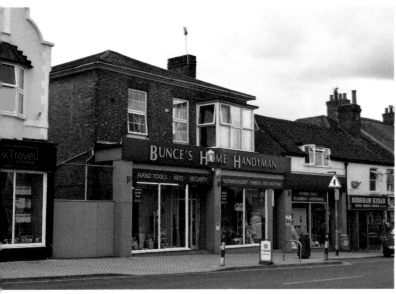

Above: The Blue Idol, founded by William Penn.

Left: Bunce's was Horsham's first police station, before Barttelot Road was built.

was Arthur Thistlewood, who was imprisoned at Horsham in 1818 for challenging the then Home Secretary, Henry Addington, to a duel. Two years later, after his release, Thistlewood was executed for treason for being a plotter in the Cato Street Conspiracy.

A bizarre thing happened in October 1785 when a shark that had been captured off the coast of Brighton was preserved and put on public display in Horsham Gaol.

Horsham has a proud history of female empowerment. Anne Briggs, a doctor working at the gaol in 1708, was revered by both the gaolers and prisoners alike for her care and skills in treating the many illnesses that afflicted people who were kept in such unhealthy conditions.

H

Horses? Or Horsa?

One very popular legend is that the name 'Horsham' has remained unchanged since its first recording in AD 947. This is partially true, though the spelling and pronunciation has varied over the past millennium. There are also two popular theories as to the origin of the name. The first says that it is derived from the Old English as a place that horses were kept, whereas the second states that it comes from a Saxon chief called Horsa. It would appear that the former theory has more credence. In his 1914 book *The Place-Names of Sussex*, Richard Roberts indicates that the spelling of Horsham was consistent from AD 947 through to 1454, albeit losing its Saxon-era accent above

Welcome to Horsham. Or should it be Horse Ham?

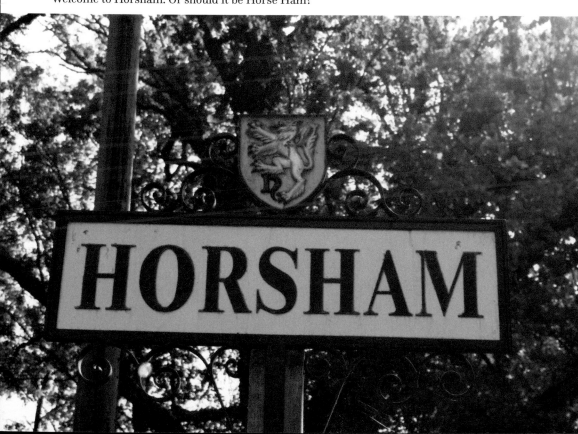

the 'a' sometime between the tenth and thirteenth centuries. It is the presence of this accent that supports the theory of being named after the animal as opposed to a person. Interestingly, it also shows the pronunciation of the name as being different to how it is said today: Hors-ham as opposed to Horsh-um. In the 1906 book *Sussex*, Wilfrid Ball notes that until as recently as the 1870s or 1880s, Horsham was known exclusively as Hors-ham, and that it was not until the railway started to bring non-locals unfamiliar with the name to the town did the pronunciation start to become the now familiar Horsh-um, and by 1906 the original (and correct) pronunciation had all but disappeared. This is supported by Arthur Stanley Cooke, writing in around 1923, who states that the correct pronunciation is Hors-ham. Other places in Sussex have retained their Saxon-era pronunciation, such as Bosham (Bos-ham), which also lends credibility to this. Further evidence of this can be found in variations to spellings recorded between 1250 and 1833 that included 'Horsam' and even 'Horseham'.

A Horsham can also be found in Pennsylvania in the USA and in Victoria, Australia. Both of these towns took their name from the Sussex Horsham. Elsewhere in the UK, a Horsham can be found in Worcestershire and Devon, Horsham St Faith can be found in Norfolk and there is a Horsham Marsh in Kent.

I

Invasion

Several 'invasions' of one sort or another have either occurred, or were planned to occur, in Horsham throughout the centuries. The first was in July 1648, when a Parliamentarian cavalry regiment of Sir Michael Livesay stormed the town to claim it from the Royalists during the English Civil War. The skirmish ended in street-to-street fighting over several hours. One soldier and three citizens of the town were killed in the invasion: Edward Filder was killed when a sword plunged through his window, William Baker was killed in some hop gardens, and Thomas Marshall was chased into East Street before being killed. The soldier appears to have been John Michell. It is reported that the victorious Parliamentarian forces were disorderly in their conduct and plundered the town, including from their own supporters. In 1644, a similar event occurred at nearby Nuthurst, when the locals killed two soldiers in defence.

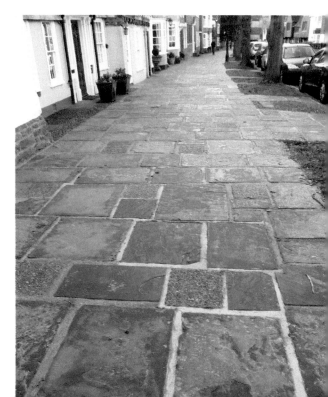

Remains of pimple sockets in
The Causeway.

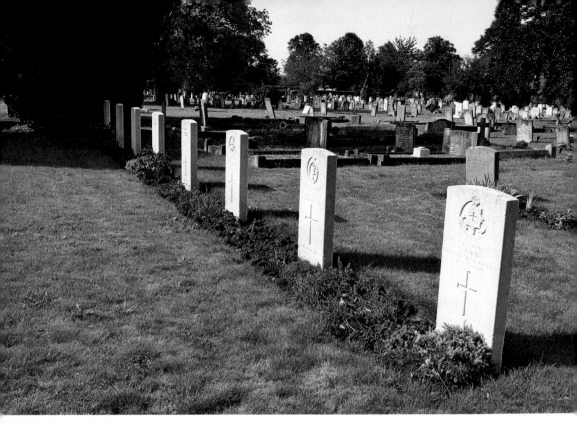

Not all of the 'friendly invaders' came home safely.

A more 'friendly invasion' happened on 10 September 1914, when 6,300 men of the 56th (1st London) Division marched through the town in a six-hour procession. They spent the night there, before moving off the following morning en route to the trenches. However, less friendly individuals in Sussex also gained the attention of the authorities, and although no reports of German spies could be found for Horsham, MI5 compiled a list of persons to be arrested in the event of a German invasion, which included Henry Anglehart, of Beaumont Lodge in nearby Ifield Wood. Others in the wider Horsham District were Dr von Muller, of Wiston Old Rectory, and Hermann Taglow, of Eltham House, Station Road, Billingshurst.

In 1940, the threat of yet another German invasion was a real prospect, and the town was designated a Category A Nodal Point, meaning that it was heavily fortified against tanks and infantry, retained a permanent garrison of regular troops alongside the Home Guard, and was expected to hold off the invader long enough until it could be relieved. Several pieces of evidence can be seen today of these anti-invasion measures, including the remains of the so-called 'dragons teeth' (or more accurately, 'pimples') in The Causeway, a pillbox near St Mary's Church, more pimples at the end of Chesworth Lane, and some anti-tank cylinders in the river next to the Denne Road tunnel. A small number of other infantry and anti-tank pillboxes still survive in and around the town, though all are on private land. While MI5 had their own arrest list of Nazi sympathisers (see the chapter on fascism), the Germans also created an arrest list of anti-Nazis, which became known as the

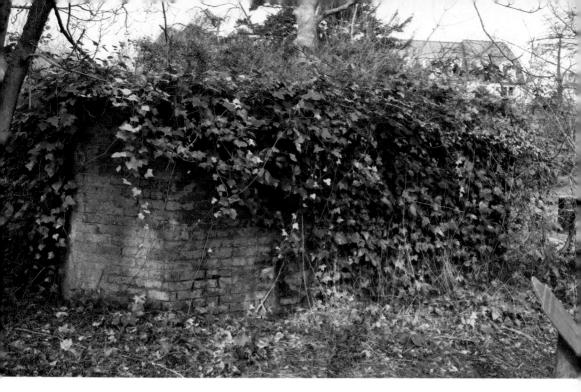

Above: The pillbox near the church is slowly disappearing from view.

Right: Surviving pimples in Chesworth Lane.

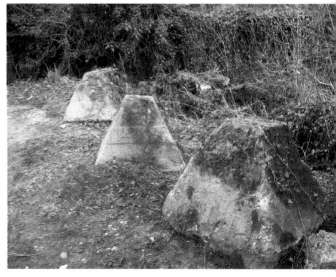

Black Book. Again, no one from Horsham itself was on the list, but Ivor Cooper, of the Old School House in nearby Rudgwick, was. The Black Book states he was a member of the 'British Armaments Committee', a senior employee at Unilever (a particular target for the Gestapo) and was noted as being 'one of the most prominent haters of Germany'. Upon invasion, he was to be tracked down, arrested and handed over to Office III of the *Reichssicherheitshauptamt* Department D2 (Commerce, Trade and Transport), headed by SS officer and convicted war criminal Willi Seibert, the deputy-commander of the notorious *Einsatzgruppe D*.

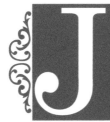

Jubilee Fountain

Tucked away in North Street between an estate agent and the council offices is the Jubilee Fountain that was originally erected in the Carfax to commemorate Queen Victoria's diamond jubilee in 1897. It was dismantled and removed from the Carfax

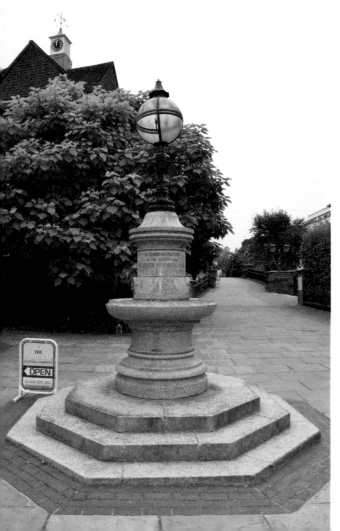

The Jubilee Fountain.

in 1947 when it became a traffic hazard, being isolated in the middle of the road. It spent many years stuck in Horsham Park (some say in a state of disrepair) where the volleyball courts north of Park House are today, until, after much campaigning, it was restored and placed on a verge on the south side of Copnall Way (south of the RSA Building today) in 1977, being inscribed with another dedication to the present queen's silver jubilee. It was moved again in the early 1990s, when that part of the Carfax/North Street was redeveloped, to its present position. That it still survives is fortunate, since one potential plan in 1947 was for its permanent demolition.

That it even existed in the first place was in doubt since it was just one of four proposals to mark the event. Plans to commemorate the jubilee were first put forward in 1887, and initially favoured a cottage hospital. Another proposal was a Queen Victoria Memorial Hall, a triangular-shaped building to have been built on Gaol Green (the part of the Carfax where the Bandstand is today), perhaps to replace the town hall. As it happened, both the fountain and the cottage hospital (built in 1892, and still used today as part of the larger Horsham Hospital in Hurst Road) were erected. The sixty-eighth birthday of Queen Victoria in 1887 was less well celebrated, with just two shops in West Street displaying a penny flag each, and one house having the Union Flag hoisted to half mast.

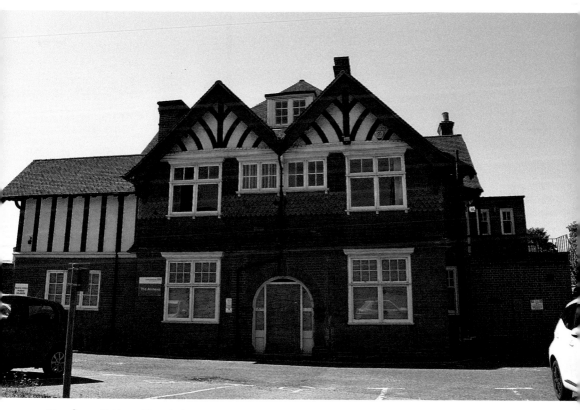

Horsham Cottage Hospital.

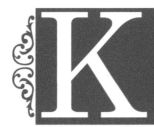

King and Barnes

With its foundations dating as far back as 1800, a number of mergers of town breweries eventually resulted in the once well-known and highly popular King and Barnes forming in 1906, and becoming the last surviving Horsham brewery. Today, little of it physically remains, with only a small part of the brewery site in the Bishopric surviving the demolition when the company was sold to Hall and

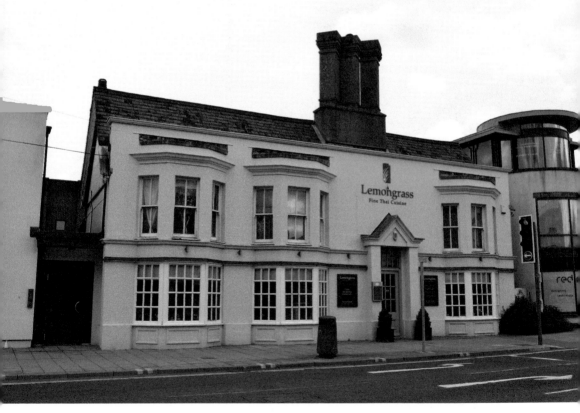

All that remains of the King and Barnes Brewery.

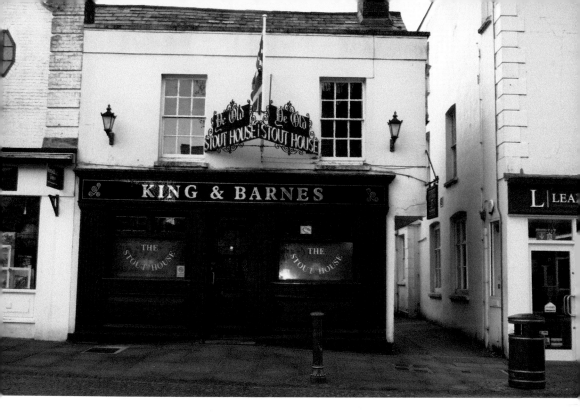

Above: Ye Old Stout House still bears the King and Barnes name.

Right: The much-loved bear at The Bear, a former King and Barnes pub.

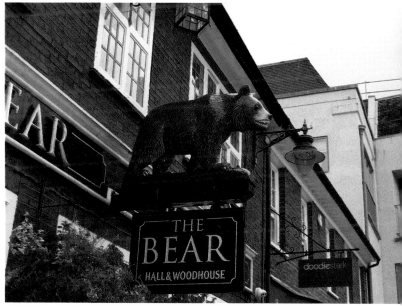

Woodhouse and the building sold to a housing developer in 2000. The King and Barnes offices also used to stand at the north end of the Carfax, though these too have been demolished. However, Ye Old Stout House, a short distance away, still retains the King and Barnes name on its wall, and several other former King and Barnes pubs exist under the Hall and Woodhouse name.

Langhurst Wood: Seventy Years of Secrets

Established in 1941 when some 80 acres around Langhurst House were requisitioned by the government, the area known as Langhurst Wood became a top-secret experimental facility for testing new weapons, becoming the Petroleum Warfare Department (PWD) in 1942. A number of flame warfare weapons were developed and tested at Langhurst between 1942 and 1946, including rockets, flame fougasse, infantry flamethrowers, sea flame barrages, and the Wasp and Churchill Crocodile tanks used on D-Day. Langhurst was also where Operation PLUTO was developed to transport oil across the Channel after D-Day. The Special Operations Executive was known to train at Langhurst from

The entrance to the original Langhurst Wood research site.

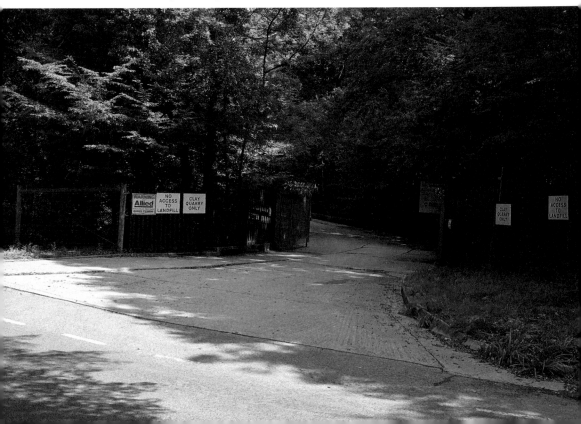

time to time. The PWD was dissolved after the war, but Langhurst continued to be used by the military. In March and April 1967, flamethrowers and other incendiary devices developed at Langhurst (by then called the Royal Armament Research and Development Establishment) were used during the SS *Torrey Canyon* disaster; a declassified film of this is now freely available on YouTube.

The site closed in 1975, being used by other branches of the armed forces on a temporary basis until finally being abandoned in 1978. In February 1980, the Home Office took over the site to open the Scientific Advisory Branch – a top-secret research facility working on crime prevention and defence. More recently, the site (now moved to a 26-acre high-security site on the north of Langhurst Wood Road and known as the Centre for Applied Science and Technology) had been used to develop such things as body armour and checkpoint surveillance, and was integrated with the Defence Science and Technology Laboratory at Porton Down on 1 April 2018.

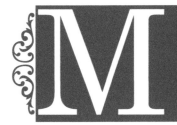

Manor House

There have been many manors in and around Horsham, but this book will focus on one that, although highly visible in the town centre, is perhaps one of the least known. Hewells Manor in The Causeway was first mentioned in 1532 as part of Rusper Priory. Upon the dissolution of the monasteries it passed to Robert and Margaret Southwell, then in turn variously to Henry Foyce, John Hall and finally to John Ravenscroft, until the latter's death in 1615 when it was absorbed into the rectory estate. In 1704, the manor was sold by Elizabeth Delves to Nathaniel Tredcroft, who rebuilt the house as the one that we still see today, appearing to lose the name of Hewells and simply becoming the Manor House. He died in 1720 and Hewells passed down the line of inheritance until Edward Tredcroft sold it to Henry Padwick in 1856. Padwick died in 1916 and it initially passed to his widow, Jane Elenor Padwick, who then sold it later that year. The manor became a school, established by Mr H. N. Layton in 1919, until it closed in 1970, by which time a purpose-built school had been constructed in the grounds away from the main house (where Sainsbury's is today). It was then purchased by the RSPCA to become their national headquarters in 1973 and remained so until 2003 when they moved out to new purpose-built headquarters at Southwater. Tanbridge School merged with the former Manor House School in 1976. In 1990 this school closed and Tanbridge moved to its present location and the land sold to Sainsbury's. In 2001, Horsham District Council granted permission to partly demolish sections of the Manor House (the more recent additions) and to convert it

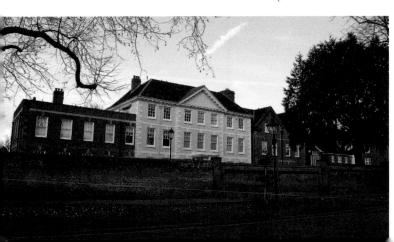

Hewells Manor, once the RSPCA headquarters and now private apartments.

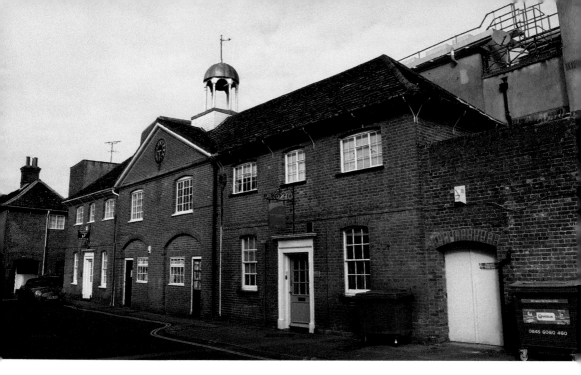

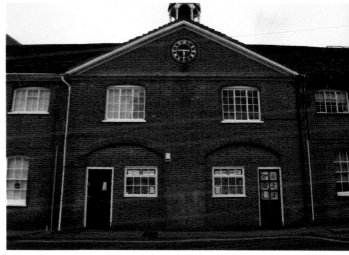

Above: The former stables and groom's quarters of Hewells Manor.

Right: The coach entrance to the former stables, now home to Willow Haven.

into eight luxury apartments, and to build a further eleven apartments and fourteen townhouses in the grounds immediately behind the house, with the first properties being sold in October 2003 for between £400,000 and £440,000. The remainder of the manor gardens were redeveloped into the present library and The Forum. In the 1970s, Blackhorse Way was built through the northern edge of the manor grounds, separating the buildings on the north side of the road from the house itself. These buildings were once the stables and grooms' quarters, now converted into shops. The main stable block, with its belfry, still retains the double archway that once allowed the carriages to enter and exit. The arches were blocked up and the space inside is now occupied by the wonderful Willow Haven shop, which is itself well worth a visit!

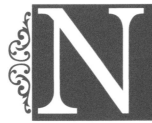

Nazi Salute at Horsham

The name for this chapter is from a *West Sussex County Times* headline in 1938, when it published a photo of a group of fifteen people conducting a Nazi salute in front of the town's war memorial. This was not someone's idea of a joke, but something that

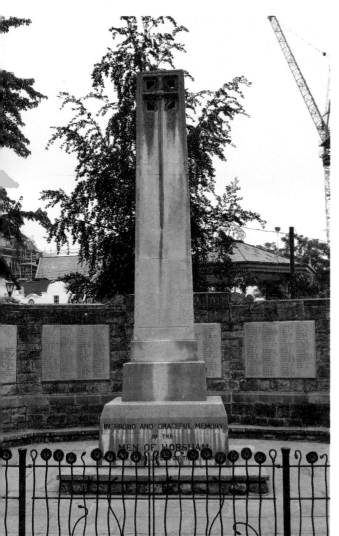

The war memorial was originally located at the large tree, east of NatWest.

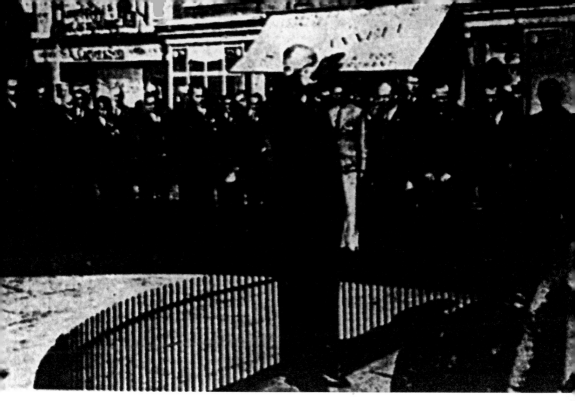

Baron Wilhelm von Lersner gives the Nazi salute at the war memorial, (WSCT photo)

was actually welcomed by the town. The origins of the story go back to August 1937 when a contingent of the Horsham Royal British Legion visited Germany to forge ties with veteran organisations in the country. The following year, the German hosts were invited to visit Horsham. The visitors comprised Baron Wilhelm von Lersner, Dr Joachim Givens, Otto August Stier, Karl Schumann, Arthur Alfred Metzsching, Wilhelm Gottlieb Kurz, Elisabetha Kurz, Wilhelm Bussmann, Johannes Bahlke, Hermann Freudenberge, Fritz Kemmerling, Alfred Wilmes, Wilhelm Klumb, Max Ernst Cuntz and Otto Wittgen. Of these, Max Cuntz was a lawyer who was implicated in the removal of Jews from the legal professions in 1933 and who, also in 1933, was involved in the seizing of assets of non-Aryans in Frankfurt. Otto Wittgen was also a full Nazi Party member who had been appointed as the acting mayor of Coblenz by Hermann Göring on 16 March 1933, becoming the full mayor of the city on 4 August. He served as the Nazi Party mayor until 1939. It was only two weeks after his appointment as mayor that attacks on, and boycotting of, Jewish citizens in the city was instigated. He also inaugurated the Adolf Hitler Bridge in 1934 and awarded Hitler 'honorary citizenship' of the city later that year.

The group arrived at Horsham on 20 August 1938 for an eight-day visit, staying at the Black Horse Hotel (now demolished, but formerly stood at the western end of West Street) throughout their visit. On the first night the Horsham RBL hosted a welcome dinner that began with toasts to the king and to the führer and concluded with the singing of the British and German national anthems. On 21 August, the German guests laid a wreath at the town war memorial in the Carfax. At the conclusion of a

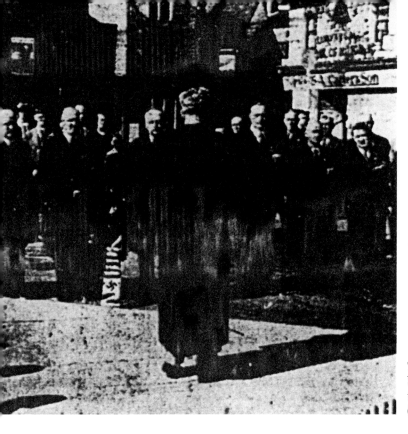

The swastika wreath
being readied at
the war memorial.
(WSCT photo)

short service by the vicar, the visitors lined up facing the memorial and Baron von Lersner placed the wreath at the foot of the memorial, followed by all fifteen giving a Nazi salute. The wreath was decorated with a swastika and the words (in German) 'To the fallen British comrades from the National-Socialist [Nazi] Maintenance Society of German ex-Servicemen'.

During the stay, the group visited London, Windsor, Eton, Brighton, Chichester, Petworth, Tonbridge, Arundel and the Kings Arms at Billingshurst. On 23 August they went to the Hurst Hut (just off Chichester Terrace) to learn the game of darts. On their final day, 27 August, the group had a farewell dinner at Hurst Hut, during which Baron von Lersner presented the Horsham RBL with a swastika pennant, which was duly affixed to the Legion's standard, and the branch returned the favour by appointing von Lersner and Otto Wittgen as honorary members of the Horsham branch. It is reported that as the train left Horsham station that evening, a crowd of several hundred people turned out to see them off, singing 'Auld Lang Syne' as the train departed.

O

Old Town Hall

Adding the prefix 'old' to the town hall is a point of contention for some, owing to the fact that, although now long since disused for that purpose, there has not been a 'new' town hall. However, I am opting to use the prefix in this book, since that is how the building is popularly and affectionately known, and that the word 'old' has been used to describe the town hall since at least 1888, from when the present building partly dates. A town hall on the spot dates back to the sixteenth century, when it was a typical Sussex-style building – square, with an upper chamber elevated by arches so that

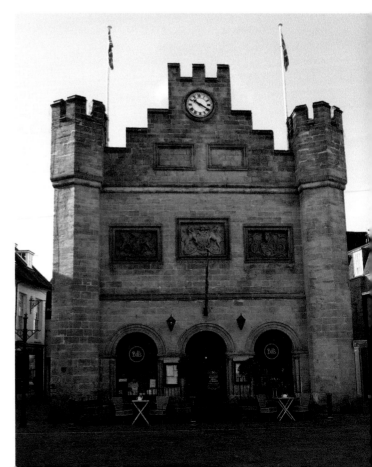

The Old Town Hall.

markets could be held underneath. This would have been used for many purposes, including for the town assizes, a history that lasted until the magistrates court finally left in 1974. There were no cells or docks in those days, and the accused all huddled together, each awaiting his or her turn to be tried.

It was the open nature of the ground-level space that led, it is reported, to some jokers one night unloading a wagon of paving slabs that had been parked nearby for the night, dismantling the wheels, re-assembling the wagon under the town hall and then carefully loading it with the paving slabs again, trapping it under the building for some poor person to have to do the reverse actions in the morning to retrieve the wagon.

In early 1800, the town hall was extended and partly rebuilt to make it more suitable for the ongoing use of the assizes. The wooden steps were replaced with stone steps and a tower was built in the north to provide extra rooms. The first cells were then created in the basement of the tower. Three were provided, with the eastern one being for males, the western one for females, and the central, windowless cell for condemned prisoners. One of the earliest uses of this improved town hall was for a public meeting on 22 May 1800, to offer thanksgiving for the failed attempt to assassinate King George III.

More alterations were required by 1808, and the Duke of Norfolk (as owner of the building, and almost all of Horsham at the time) proposed to further enlarge it, or perhaps build a new town hall. The former plan was approved by the magistrates. A public meeting was held on 20 July 1812 to discuss the improvements, which unanimously approved the idea, not least due to the offer of the Duke of Norfolk to personally pay for the works. The improvements were made by April 1813. It was these works that resulted in the castle-like north façade of the building, with its two corner turrets and carvings of the Royal Arms, the Arms of the Duke of Norfolk and the Arms of Horsham.

In May 1887, attention once again turned to the state of the building, which had been condemned as unsafe, the west side being close to complete collapse. Repair was considered unsatisfactory and so the Local Board instead voted to demolish it

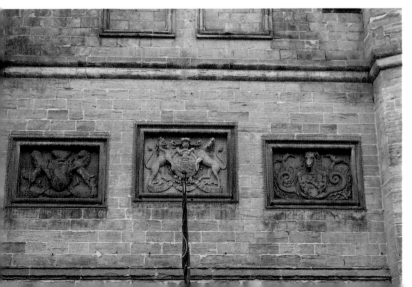

The arms of the Duke of Norfolk, the Crown and Horsham.

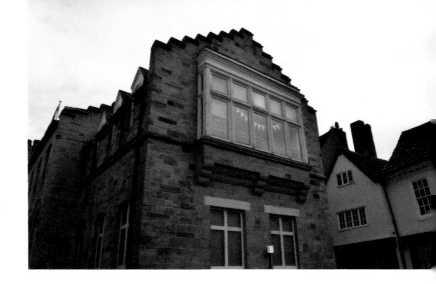

The 1889 extension was highly sympathetic to the original 1812 structure.

and build a new town hall in its place. This was met with horror by several businesses in Market Square, not because of the proposed demolition, but because of the plans to build a larger hall in its place. They claimed it would bring it too close to existing buildings and instead suggested that a new hall be built on Gaol Green. By this time, the hall had become the property of the town. Work began in late 1888 on what was to become the town hall we know today. The idea of complete demolition was an exaggeration, since the 1812-era north face was retained, and evidence suggests the eastern side is also largely original to 1812. It would appear that just the south and west sides were rebuilt, and the works were completed by mid-1889. The basement was remodelled in late 1909, when the six wooden cells were created. For much of the 2000s, the town hall was used for occasional exhibitions but was mostly left disused, other than the registry office that existed in the building. In 2012, to much protest, permission was granted for Bills Restaurant to open in the town hall, but has since become an established and well-used venue.

The Old Town Hall was also the scene of another historic event, when on 2 July 1814 a public meeting of the townspeople voted to petition for the end of slavery. A second anti-slavery petition was sent to the Commons on 16 April 1833, so clearly this was an issue that Horsham refused to give up on.

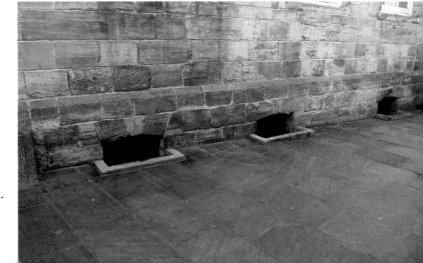

The town hall basement, where criminals awaited their turn in the dock.

Plague

Horsham did not escape the plague pandemics that spread across Britain and Europe in centuries past. In fact, the town was hit multiple times between 1560 and 1610. Of one outbreak in 1574, no records could be found, but a curious note in the baptism entry of 24 September states that Jane Clerke had to be baptised in Warnham on that date, because 'ye plague was then in this parishe [i.e. Horsham]'. Margaret Wright had to be baptised at Warnham on 6 October for the same reason, and Henry Fist and Mary Voice were both baptised in Itchingfield (on 5 November and 10 December, respectively) because of the plague in Horsham. An identical note is beside the marriage entry for John Pillfold and Joan Pyck, who had to marry at Itchingfield for the same reason. In the later outbreaks, an isolated victim of the disease was Agnes Collingborne, who was buried at St Mary's churchyard on 9 May 1604. The final epidemic began in February 1609, when Blanch Dungate was the first recorded victim, being buried on 28 February. A further eight people succumbed in March (accounting for half of all the townspeople to die that month), including a mother and daughter within just two days of each other. This increased to twenty-seven people in April 1609, most of whom were children, and thirteen in May. A particular tragedy struck the Pledge household when three of the children all died and were buried on the same day. Between February 1609 and March 1610, seventy-seven Horsham residents had died of the plague. Another eight victims were buried in 1610, with the last being John Alleyn (another child victim) on 27 November.

POW Camps

A number of prison camps were established in and around Horsham in both world wars. The first, formed within a week of war being declared on 4 August 1914, was at Christ's Hospital School. This was an emergency camp to take German prisoners in the very early stages of the war before permanent prisons had been established. The first contingent of prisoners were eighty-five German army reservists arrested in Kent trying to sail back to Europe, a number of German nationals arrested at Dover,

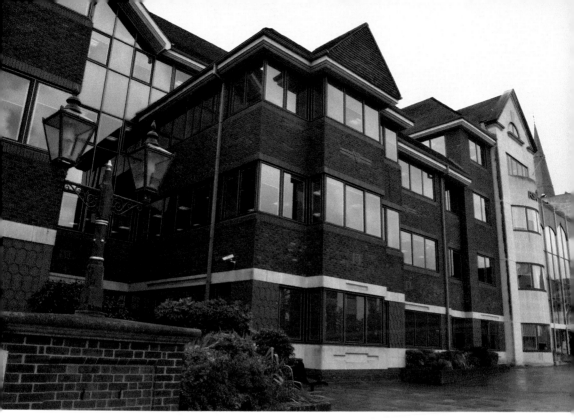

No. 18 North Street stood here until demolished in the 1980s.

several suspected spies and the surviving crews of two German ships that had been captured. One of these was the SS *Königin Luise*, which had the duel notoriety of having sunk the first British ship and for being the first German ship lost in the war. The camp was short lived, but by the end of the month 400 prisoners had passed through it before being transferred to Edinburgh. There were rumours of a section of the grounds remaining as a camp once the school re-opened in September 1914, though this did not happen.

A second prison camp was established for twenty-five German prisoners at the very end of the war on 23 February 1918, at what was No. 18 North Street – a large house demolished in the 1980s for the RSA building. These prisoners were to work on local farms, with their horses being stabled at the old West Street Brewery from the end of March 1918. In June, the brewery itself was put up for sale by Rice Brothers, and it would appear that it was purchased by the military authorities, since in the first week of September 1918 it was taken over as a prison camp to house 100 Germans, the North Street property having been given up as too small. By May 1919, the scale of the camp had reduced, and a sale of horses and other camp equipment was held, although there were still some German prisoners 'residing' at the site. It would appear that the last of the prisoners were removed by November 1919, and the site ceased to be a prison camp.

In the Second World War, a prison camp was situated in Marringdean Road, Billingshurst, with a number of smaller satellite camps established around West Sussex, with the closest one to Horsham at Coolhurst. In fact, there were two camps

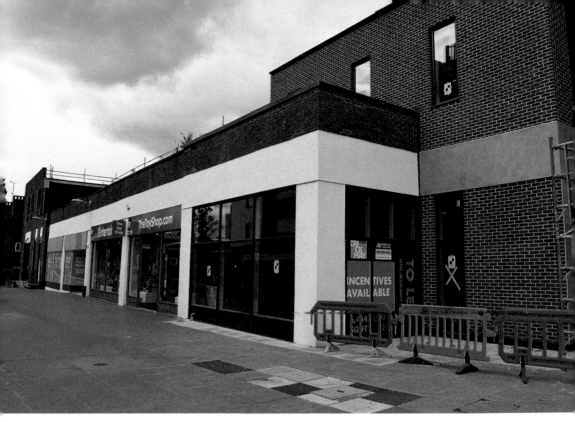

These shops stand on the same footprint as the West Street Brewery.

here, with Camp No.1 (thirty huts) located behind St John's Church and Camp No.2 (seventeen huts) adjoining the north side of Coolhurst House. Sources differ as to the composition of the prisoners, with most stating that the Coolhurst camps were used for Italians, and a single source stating that Eastern Europeans in German service were also held there.

Qui Vive Corps: Horsham's Own Suffragettes

Originally the Marchers' Qui Vive Corps, this organisation was formed following a 466-mile women's march from Edinburgh to Downing Street in November 1912, led by Florence de Fonblanque. The aim of the Corps was, among other things, to show that women were just as capable as men of organisation, comradeship and discipline.

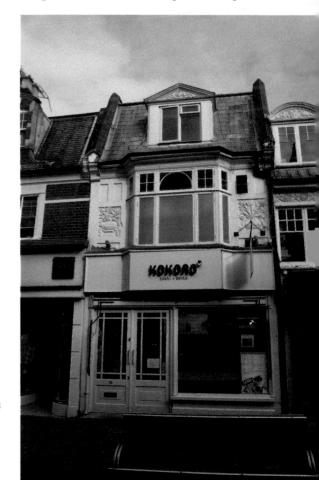

No. 60 West Street, once the headquarters of two suffrage organisations.

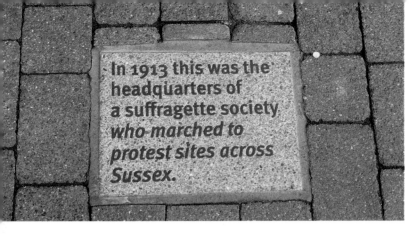

Commemorative plaque in West Street – except it is outside the wrong building!

Members were both militant and non-militant, though they had to all pledge to not undertake militant activities when dressed in the Corps colours (brown coat and skirt and a brown hat with emerald-green cockade). The origins of the Corps in Horsham dated to March 1913, when Mrs de Fonblanque announced at the end of a meeting of the Horsham Women's Suffrage Society (WSS) that she was inaugurating the Qui Vive Corps in the town. She opened a Qui Vive Corps depot at No. 60 West Street later that month. A plaque marking this has been placed in West Street, but at the time of writing is embarrassingly outside the wrong building! It may be relocated to the correct location during the next West Street refurbishment.

The first event came on 28 March 1913, when Mrs de Fonblanque chaired a public meeting at the town hall, with speeches by Revd Claude Hinscliff and Ruth Cavendish Bentinck. This was followed on 14 May by a two-day march from Horsham to Brighton. Upon leaving West Street, they first marched to The Causeway for speeches by Mrs de Fonblanque, Mrs Porch and Jaakoff Prelooker. The Qui Vive Corps banner was then raised and they continued the march to Brighton. They returned on the 16 May, reaching the Carfax at 7.00 p.m. for a public meeting addressed by Mrs de Fonblanque, Revd Boyle (vicar of Portslade), Margaret Elizabeth Byham, Mrs Porch, Mrs F. Kerr, Miss Jackson and Miss A. N. Roff, the meeting having been arranged by Mrs Fleming. Horsham was weary of the 'Brown Women' at first and this meeting was not well received. The crowd became agitated and hostile, and despite the best efforts of Mr Jury Cramp and Miss Byham, they were forced to leave for the railway station, accompanied by booing, laughing and cheers from the crowd, which had to be kept back by over a dozen police officers. The following morning, a boy discovered an incendiary bomb that had been left by an opponent on the doorstep of the West Street depot. It consisted of discharged fireworks in a tin, though thankfully it failed to do any damage. The local press was largely opposed to women's suffrage at the time, and on 29 May 1913, the *West Sussex Gazette* proudly exclaimed that 'Horsham is reversing the order of things, with a vengeance' after a second bomb had been discovered at the entrance to No. 60 West Street in the early hours of that morning. This one was a lead case containing a quantity of gunpowder and an unlit fuse.

This did not put off the Qui Vive Corps. On 12 April, four members (Miss Byham, Miss Roff and Mrs de Fonblanque; the fourth member is not known) marched from Horsham to Southwater to hold a small meeting, where Mrs de Fonblanque amused the

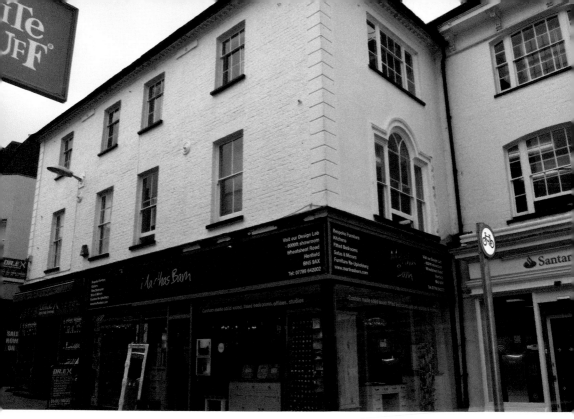

No. 5 Middle Street, home to Louisa Jane Churchman, a prominent suffragist.

audience with anecdotes from the Edinburgh–London march in 1912. On the personal invitation of Lady Cowdray they next marched from Horsham to Cowdray Park on 1 August 1913, reaching Midhurst the following morning. Another public meeting was held on 27 August at the town hall, chaired by Mrs de Fonblanque. Speeches were given by Miss Roff and Louisa Jane Churchman (the latter living at No. 5 Middle Street, and a member of the Horsham WSS) and a sizeable collection was taken. Mrs de Fonblanque and Miss Roff spoke again at an open-air meeting that evening.

The Qui Vive Corps gave up their West Street depot at the end of September 1913 (when it was taken over by the Horsham WSS), with the headquarters moving to Mrs de Fonblanque's Duncton home. The last recorded event of the Qui Vive Corps in Horsham was due to have been on 28 August 1914, when they intended to complete a combined total of 1,000 miles of marches since 1912 by walking from Bournemouth to Horsham. It is doubtful whether this happened, since war broke out on 4 August.

Horsham Women's Suffrage Society

As mentioned above, Horsham also had a separate Women's Suffrage Society, which was the largest suffrage organisation in the town, with colours of green, white and red. On 20 January 1910, a National Union of Women's Suffrage Societies (NUWSS) meeting was held at the King's Head, presided over by Mr A. C. Holland and

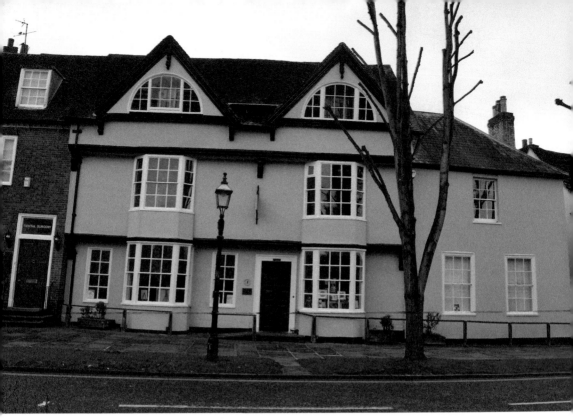

Causeway House, now Horsham Museum, home to Lettice Arnold, a Horsham suffragist.

supported by Mrs Hurst (of Horsham Park), Mrs Osborne, Mrs Fyffe (of The Capite, West Grinstead), Mrs and Miss Churchman, Miss Weir (of No. 17 Richmond Road), Miss Pirouet, Mr Jury Cramp and Miss Sayers. Speakers were Miss M. F. Basden (of Brighton and Hove WSS) and Miss A. S. Verrell. The meeting attracted so large a crowd that there was not even standing room in the hall. At the meeting, Lettice Arnold (of Causeway House, now Horsham Museum), announced that petitions would be posted outside polling booths at the upcoming council elections. A general election had also been held in January, and although the Liberal candidate, R. L. Outhwaite, had stated pre-election that he favoured women's suffrage, *The Vote* reported afterwards that both he and the winning Conservative candidate were hostile to the issue. At the election, the petition managed to gain 411 signatures from Horsham voters.

The Horsham WSS itself was founded at an inaugural meeting at Horsham Park (now Park House) on 29 June 1910, becoming the town's first suffrage organisation. Barbara Duncan, Miss Merryfield (in the chair) and Mrs Robie Uniacke all spoke at the meeting and a vote was taken to form a branch. The first committee was formed in early July, namely Mrs Hurst (chairman) and Mrs Keatinge (honorary secretary; widow of R. H. Keatinge VC). Their first committee meeting was held on 6 July, and on 8 July their first public meeting was held in the Carfax, presided over by Sir Eustace Piers, Barbara Duncan and Mrs Stansbury. It was also in July 1910 that Mrs Fyffe resigned her position as vice-president of the Women's National Liberal Association (a post she held for seventeen years) and as president of the Horsham Women's

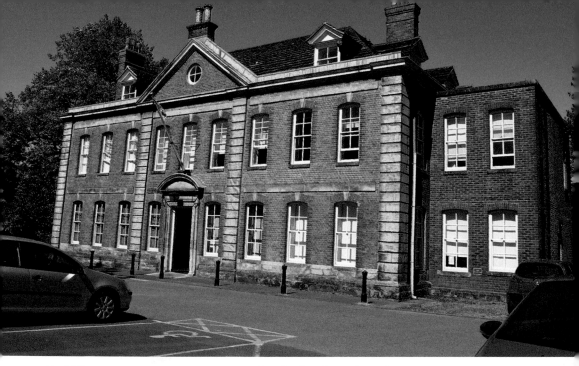

Park House on 29 June 2018 – 108 years after the founding of Horsham WSS.

Liberal Association in protest of the Party's attitude to suffrage. Louisa Churchman had recently been made treasurer of the Horsham WLA, but she also resigned in protest. At the end of the month, the Horsham WSS became affiliated to Millicent Fawcett's NUWSS as part of its Surrey, Sussex and Hampshire Federation, and on 29 October 1910 the branch took part in the NUWSS demonstration through Guildford city centre. This was followed on 31 October by a private meeting at Lynwood, the home of Mrs Keatinge (a demolished house on the site of Nos 7–28 Ravenscroft Court, at the corner of Rushams Road and North Parade). A number of smaller, semi-public meetings were held throughout the winter at Hanley's Temperance Hotel.

The New Year for the Horsham WSS began on 19 January 1911, when Sir Eustace Piers held a meeting of Horsham voters to educate and interest the town in women's suffrage, and to get a petition to send to parliament. The first annual meeting was on 8 July 1911 at the town hall, where Lord Robert Cecil was guest speaker, aided by Mrs Hurst, Mr and Mrs Maurice Keatinge, Miss Hutchings, Miss Bradburne (treasurer), Miss Coleman, Lettice Arnold and Sir Eustace Piers. By now, the branch had sixty-one members.

A Carfax meeting was held on 24 May 1912 by Norah O'Shea (secretary of the Surrey, Sussex and Hampshire Federation), Mr H. Rolleston Stables and Mrs Lyall Dempster (by now the branch chairman). Mrs Dempster and Miss O'Shea addressed another Carfax meeting on 24 June. That year's annual meeting came on 26 September at the town hall, where Maude Royden was the speaker, presided over by Lady Farrer. Several new members joined up after the meeting, and Miss Royden hosted a public meeting at the same venue later that evening.

On 17 October 1912, Mrs Fyffe organised a march and protest at Whiteley's Auction Rooms at Westbourne Grove, London, where her goods were being sold off after they

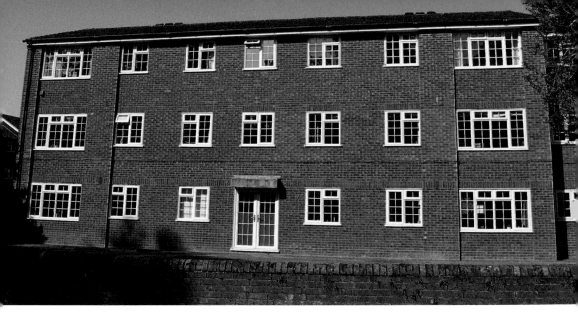

The site of Lynwood, former home to Mrs and General Keatinge VC.

were seized when she refused to pay her taxes – she having become the treasurer of the Women's Tax Resistance League in addition to her position on the committee of the Horsham WSS. Ten days later, Dr Drysdale and Miss Royden addressed three separate Horsham WSS meetings.

The 1913 annual meeting was held at the Black Horse Hotel on 3 July, chaired by the Hon. Lady Johnstone and addressed by Sir William Chance and Norah O'Shea. It was on 29 September 1913 that the Horsham WSS also took over the No. 60 West Street depot of the Qui Vive Corps, which they turned into a Women's Social and Literary Club and reading room, where meetings and debates were held weekly on Thursdays. When the First World War broke out in 1914, the branch made a public appeal for fruit, sugar and jars to make jam that could be distributed to the town's poor during the winter. The depot was transformed into a jam factory and enough donations were made to produce 200 lbs of jam. Suffrage organisations appear to have stopped using the West Street depot in 1915, when it became the Southern Printing Co.

The Surrey, Sussex and Hampshire Federation itself held a bulb sale in Horsham to raise funds, and Mrs Earle, Miss Bateson and Miss Case gave lectures on gardening. A total of £8 16s (2019: £519) was raised. Three days later, Mrs Dempster held another branch meeting at No. 60 West Street.

Unlike the other suffrage organisations that existed in the town, the Horsham WSS continued to campaign throughout the war years. Perhaps the biggest event in the branch's history came on 22 March 1915, when they hosted the NUWSS president and leading suffragist, Millicent Fawcett, at the Black Horse Assembly Rooms on the subject of the women's movement in relation to the war. At the end of the year, a bed at a Serbian military hospital was named 'Horsham' after being sponsored by the Horsham WSS. The branch also donated to other Serbian hospital units, as well as to hospital units for Russian refugees in 1916. Wartime work was also closer to home, with several women members of the town's suffrage organisations (and others

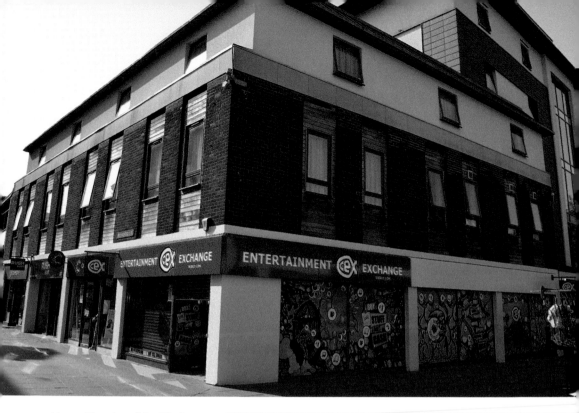

Above: The site of the Black Horse, where Millicent Fawcett visited in 1915.

Right: Memorial to the town's women at the War Hospital Supply Depot.

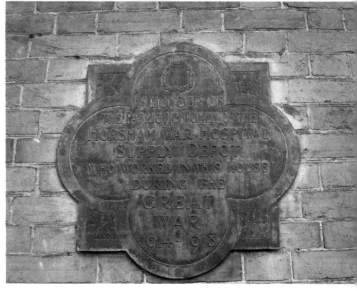

who were not) setting up the Horsham War Hospital Supply Depot at Nos 7–8 The Causeway, which made items, such as bandages, for use at the war hospital to treat wounded soldiers. Mrs Hurst, Mrs Keatinge, Miss Churchman and Miss Arnold were all known to be among those involved with the Depot in one form or another. It was also Southern Printing Co. (at No. 60 West Street) that sold tickets to a Grand Fete at the Manor House (Hewells) in 1918 to raise money for the Depot.

The Horsham WSS dissolved in 1918 upon some women gaining the vote, becoming re-named the Horsham Women Citizens' Association, which continued to campaign for equal suffrage. This then became the Horsham Townswomen's Guild in the 1930s after equal suffrage was achieved in 1928. The Horsham Guild survived until at least 1954.

Mrs Keatinge, of Lynwood, was the first Horsham WSS secretary from 29 June 1910 to March 1911. Next was Lettice Arnold, of Causeway House, from March 1911 to January 1912. Mrs Keatinge had a second term from January to March 1912. She was succeeded by Louisa Churchman, of No. 5 Middle Street, from March 1912 to April 1913. The fifth honorary secretary was Mrs Blackburn, initially of No. 35 Gladstone Road then No. 3 Rushams Road, from January 1913 as co-secretary with Miss Churchman and as full secretary from April 1913 until July 1913. Next was Miss Rowe, of Chestnut Lodge (Pondtail Road) from July 1913 to February 1915. Louisa Churchman had a second term from February 1915 until at least September 1916. Miss Knight, of Rapkyns (now a care home off Guildford Road, Broadbridge Heath) joined Miss Churchman as co-secretary from February 1915 until at least September 1916, which is the last date that references can be found.

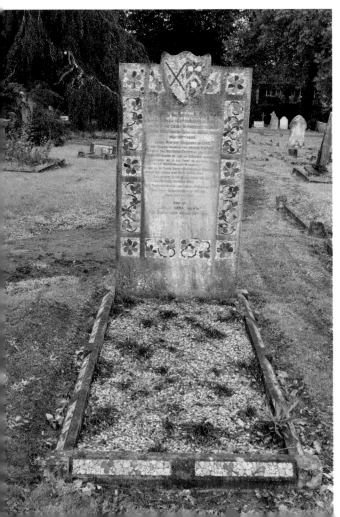

Keatinge grave at Hills.
Mrs Keatinge helped establish the
Horsham WSS.

Women's Social and Political Union

The most famous of the suffrage organisations was the militant Women's Social and Political Union, with its colours of white, green and purple, and led by the Pankhursts. Although Horsham never had its own WSPU branch, it did host several meetings. The first was on 2 October 1908, when between fifty and sixty people gathered at the Black Horse Assembly Rooms to hear Emmeline Pethick-Lawrence (who lived at Holmwood, near Dorking) and Miss Canning (of the Chelsea WSPU) speak. Both were militant suffragettes; Mrs Pethick-Lawrence was arrested six times between 1906 and 1913, including twice in 1912, and Miss Canning spent a month in Holloway. The next suffragette event was on 25 November 1908, when a lecture was given using the 'magic lantern', the early projector. On 18 January 1909, Edith New hosted a debate at Southwater church schoolroom. She was a militant member of the WSPU and was one of the first two suffragettes to use vandalism as a campaign tactic when she smashed the windows of No. 10 Downing Street in June 1908. On 17 January 1908, she had chained herself to the gates of Downing Street to allow two other suffragettes to gain entry to the building.

Mary Hare (of Brighton WSPU) was a speaker at the Southwater Debating Society on 25 January 1909, contesting Mr L. Paice on the subject of women's suffrage. Miss Hare had been selected for the task by Revd Boyd, president of the debating society. At the end of the debate, a vote of the audience was taken, with a large majority siding with Miss Hare. Another public WSPU meeting was held at the town hall on 3 February 1910, chaired by Miss Beck (of Duncans Farm, Billingshurst) and addressed by Miss Sheppard and Miss Canning (both of the Chelsea branch WSPU). An Australian newspaper dated 2 July 1912 reported receiving a cablegram from London stating that on 30 June suffragettes were suspected of attempting to burn down two houses in Horsham after kerosene-soaked paper and canvas was found and holes had been made in the doors. Two ladies were apparently seen in the vicinity in the early morning and items were found near one of the doors. No local reports could be found to corroborate this.

Two further WSPU meetings were held in Horsham in 1912, the first on 31 July in the Carfax and the second on 2 August, also in the Carfax, hosted by Lieutenant Cather (of Cavendish Road, Redhill). The Pankhursts never visited Horsham as part of the suffrage campaign, but Sylvia Pankhurst did attempt to address a badly received public meeting opposing conscription in the Carfax in 1916.

Other Suffrage Organisations

On 19 June 1908, a Women's Freedom League van visited as part of a county-wide propaganda caravan tour. On 17 November 1908, Edwin Richmond, of the Men's League for Women's Suffrage, chaired a joint meeting of the Horsham Women's Liberal Association and League of Young Liberals at the Albion Hall. Mrs Conybeare, of the Horsham WLA, spoke on the subject of women's suffrage. There was an attempt in 1909 to form a Horsham branch of the Men's League, but, it appears, without success.

The West Sussex branch of the militant Women's Freedom League held a public meeting in the Carfax on 20 September 1909. It had been advertised by a series of chalk messages on the town's pavements earlier that afternoon which read 'Votes for Women. Carfax to-night 7.30. Women's Freedom League.' Five women, including the honorary secretary Miss Cummins (daughter of the vicar of Easebourne), addressed a large crowd. The meeting was delayed by ten minutes by the Salvation Army, who were preaching and playing music in the Carfax. When the meeting began, Miss Cummins explained the purpose was to correct errors that were frequently printed in the press. There was frequent sexist heckling as she spoke and as Madge Turner took the stage she, too, was constantly interrupted by bells and laughing. She began by asking why the crowd thought women's suffrage was so amusing and that 'men wanted the vote years ago, and did worse things than [women] did'. Someone responded with 'we did not break windows and break down with hatchets', to which Miss Turner quipped 'no, but you burnt down houses'. She gave way to Mrs Arncliffe-Sennett (sister of Florence de Fonblanque), who was similarly drowned out by the noisemakers. At first, PC Sopp was the only officer present, standing in front of the stage, but as the crowd became more threatening, others were called in, including Superintendent Goldring and Sergeant Blackman, to protect the speakers. The meeting managed to last fifty-five minutes before it had to be broken up and the women were escorted by the police to Linden's Temperance Hall in North Street, followed by the baying crowd. They were then later escorted to the train station. Maud Arncliffe-Sennett attempted another Horsham meeting one week later, but was again hounded out of town by anti-suffragists.

Suffragists and Suffragettes

In addition to those mentioned previously in this chapter, the following were notable suffrage supporters in Horsham. Mr Jaakoff Prelooker (of Ifield) was charged at the Horsham Petty Sessions at the town hall on 28 March 1908 for non-payment of rates. He admitted the charge, saying that it was in protest of the fact that his household was disenfranchised – he was a foreign citizen and his wife (an Englishwoman) had no vote. After the hearing he hosted the town's first recorded suffrage event, speaking at a meeting of considerable size, aided by Edith New and Miss Lightman of the WSPU. He said he was not a suffrage supporter for any personal gain, but because women had been badly treated by men for too long.

Henry Devenish Harben (of Warnham Lodge) married Agnes Helen Bostock (of No. 7 North Street) at St Mary's Church on 2 September 1899, at which General Keatinge VC and Mrs Keatinge were guests. Agnes' father was the then chairman of Horsham Urban District Council. Both became active suffragists, but had by then moved to Ambersham. Henry had been a financier and lawyer to the WSPU and was an associate of Christabel Pankhurst. He was arrested in London on 25 February 1914. Agnes later left the WSPU and became a co-founder of the United Suffragists in

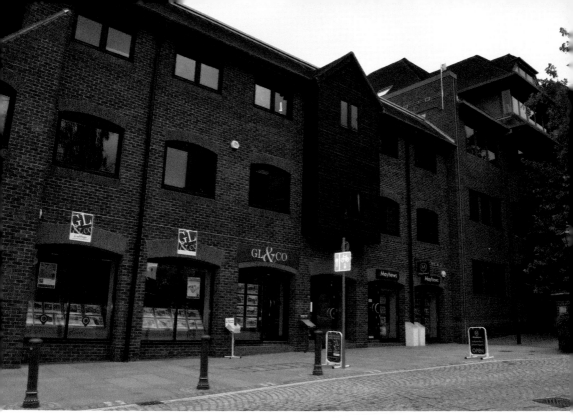

Mayhews stands on the site of Agnes Harben's North Street home.

1914 – a breakaway group that grew impatient at the lack of success of the NUWSS and opposed the arson campaign of the WSPU. It was uniquely open equally to men and women, militants and non-militants, and continued to campaign throughout the war years. Its colours were purple, white and orange. Henry also joined the United Suffragists, but continued to be a close friend of Christabel and financier of her militant organisations.

Catherine Richmond lived her later years at Comfrey, Coneyhurst Road in Coolham and was a committed Quaker. She was a former militant suffragette when she was living in Redhill and had been arrested on 25 February 1909. She died on 5 June 1939 and was the first person in over 200 years to be buried at the Blue Idol graveyard.

Kate Snelling was a non-millitant suffragist from Horsham, and was involved in raising money to build Horsham Hospital. She died in May 1948 aged seventy and was buried at Hills Cemetery. Ruth Albery was also a Horsham-based non-militant suffragist, born at No. 49 West Street (now T. H. Baker Jewellers) in 1866. She lived in Horsham until 1951 and died aged ninety-two in January 1958.

Mr Jury Cramp was the honorary secretary of Horsham Temperance Association, and was involved in many town activities at the time. He was a self-confessed life-long supporter of women's suffrage, but was deeply opposed to militant tactics. He had been present at a meeting by David Lloyd George that was attacked by suffragettes. In early 1910, he petitioned Horsham in favour of women's suffrage, but reported having difficulty due to the militant tactics of the WSPU.

Female Representation

Horsham was fairly quick at electing females post-1918. The first female councillor of Horsham Urban District Council was Nellie Vesta Laughton, elected in April 1922, who served continuously until 1951 as the only woman councillor. She retired in 1951, but Mrs Gale Moore was elected, meaning that Horsham still had a woman councillor (Mrs Moore became the very first female council chairman in 1956). It wasn't until 1952 that a second female councillor was elected. When the Urban Council became Horsham District Council in 1974, the first woman chairman came in 1977 (Avocet Frances Phelps). Since then there have been fifteen other female council chairmen, the latest being in 2015. Three women have served twice as chairmen, all between 2004 and 2011. Currently, only eight of the total forty-four district councillors are women, and only two represent wards in the town itself (which returns seventeen seats). This may change at the May 2019 elections.

In 1929, Helen Mary Keynes became the first female general election candidate for Horsham, representing Labour. She stood again in 1931. The next female candidate did not appear until 1950, and not again until 1987, when a woman candidate gained more votes than a male candidate for the first time. Next was 1992, and 1997 was the first general election where there were two female candidates for Horsham. Women candidates stood again in 2001, 2005, then not until 2015. The 2017 general election was the first time since 1931 (when there were only two candidates) that there was almost parity between the genders, with three female and four male candidates, with the women coming in second, third and fourth places. To date, Horsham has never elected a female MP, and of the fifteen parties that have fielded candidates for Horsham since women were given the vote in 1918, only five have stood female candidates: Labour and the Liberal Democrats have stood five each, and the Green Party, Liberal Party and SDP have each put forward one woman candidate.

Louisa Churchman, the former secretary of Horsham WSS, became the town's first female magistrate in May 1923. She was also the first female candidate to stand in Horsham for West Sussex County Council in 1922, but was beaten by 120 votes. Mrs Mabel Louise Lintott became Horsham's first county councillor in 1925, taking the seat that Miss Churchman had contested in 1922. Currently only one of the four Horsham seats for the county council is represented by a woman.

R

Rotten Borough: Political Corruption in Horsham

In the early eighteenth century, and well into the nineteenth century, Horsham returned two members to the Commons and the nomination of candidates and the control of votes in Horsham were entirely within the hands of the town's nobility. For much of the early history, control of the manor would guarantee seats in the Commons. In fact, until 1832, each eligible voter in Horsham had the right to effectively vote for six MPs: two for Horsham, two for Bramber and two for Sussex. However, Horsham residents denied the vote were unhappy with the state of parliamentary representation long before this, and in 1817 the tax-paying townspeople submitted a petition to parliament.

The 1847 election is perhaps the most notorious example of political corruption in Horsham. By now the vote had been opened up to more men, the candidates no longer controlled the lives and livelihoods of the voters and Horsham returned a single MP. However, the competition was just as fierce. There were stories of kidnapping, intimidation and bribery. For weeks before the election, both candidates were known to host meetings in the pubs and inns and to supply each voter with beer to earn their vote. The vote was won by Radical candidate John Jervis, the son of the then attorney-general and the total amount of bribery was estimated to have been £10,000. A petition

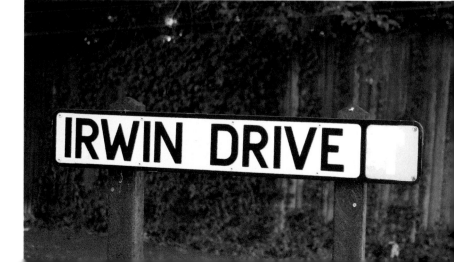

The Lords Irwin were once dominant in Horsham politics.

against the results was submitted by the Conservatives and the result was declared void owing to the bribery. A by-election was called for 1848 and William Vesey-Fitzgerald was the victor, but this resulted in another void result as more allegations of bribery were proven – including allegations that the attorney-general paid Horsham voters to return his son who had been unseated the previous year. A second by-election was called and Lord Edward Howard gained the seat for the Whigs, meaning that within a year Horsham returned three MPs from three different parties.

In 1866, allegations were again made against the result of the previous year's election, which returned Robert Henry Hurst as the Liberal MP for Horsham. The losing candidate, the Conservative Fitzgerald (who had lost out by just five votes), accused Hurst of bribery, treating voters and illegal votes. A three-day parliamentary inquiry acquitted Hurst of all charges and he kept his seat.

The 1868 election was equally fraught, when the Liberal (Hurst) and Conservative (Major Aldridge) candidates gained an equal number of votes. Unable to decide who should be elected, the returning officer announced a double return (when both were elected for the single seat) and therefore forced both candidates to challenge his opponent in the courts. Major Aldridge eventually withdrew his claim and Mr Hurst was returned as the town's MP.

In 1875, Hurst again became the MP for Horsham, having been unseated in 1874 by Fitzgerald, resulting in the last case of proven corruption in Horsham. Mr Hurst was found guilty of bribery for paying the rail fares of voters, and a by-election was duly called for 1876, when James Clifton Brown retained the seat for the Liberals, becoming the last non-Conservative MP that Horsham has returned.

Robert Henry Hurst's grave at Denne Road, now obscured by fallen trees.

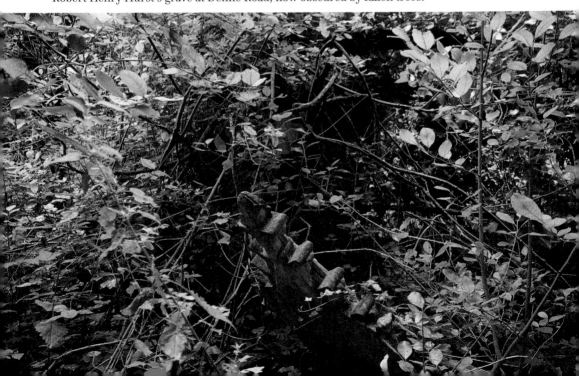

Spire of St Mark's

All that now stands of St Mark's Church is the spire isolated in the courtyard of the RSA building. The original church on the site dated to 1839, when Thomas Coppard donated enough land for both a church and graveyard to be created. Furthermore, he gave the project £50 of his own money and also donated another of his plots of land from which to quarry the stone to build the church, valued at £400. The remaining costs were raised by public subscription, and the church opened its doors in 1841. A few decades later, one of the curates had the church rebuilt at his own expense in 1870–71 and it is from this rebuild that the spire belongs. The church was demolished (except the spire) as part of a controversial town-centre redevelopment in the 1980s.

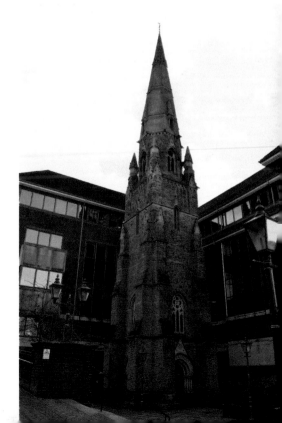

The lonely spire of St Mark's tucked away in Chart Way.

Town Mills

Horsham has long had mills producing various products. The first mention of a mill was in 1231 when a rectory mill was part of what became the Hewells Manor estate. Over the centuries this turned into what we know today as Prewett's Mill on Worthing Road. Of course, this mill has long since been used as offices and has recently been undergoing extensive redevelopment. By 1876, both Prewett's Mill and Provender Mill (known at the time as Town Mill) were producing flour. Prewett's was steam powered and Provender was water driven by a large waterwheel. Presumably Prewett's Mill would also once have been water powered, since it also stands beside the Arun. By 1911, they had both switched to milling corn. Provender Mill became disused by the 1970s, though Prewett's continued for a little while longer. A third, steam-powered, mill once existed on the site of Old Denne Gardens in Denne Road.

Security at Prewett's Mill must have been relaxed, since in October 1881, Walter Stevens was found to have 3.5 lbs of flour concealed upon his person after walking out of the mill. Stevens pleaded it was out of necessity due to having a wife and six children to feed, but only earning 17s a week as an employee of the mill. However, Mr Prewett demanded that he be charged for the theft. The police searched Stevens' house and found another 19.5 lbs of flour stolen from the mill.

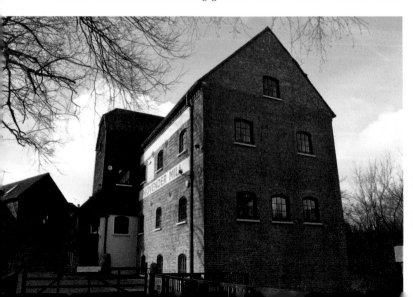

Provender Mill, once simply Town Mill, was powered by a large waterwheel.

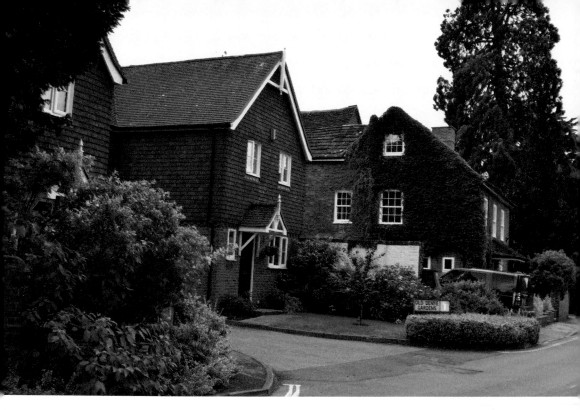

Above: The former site of a steam mill in Denne Road.

Right: Prewett's Mill, partly revealed during ongoing redevelopment.

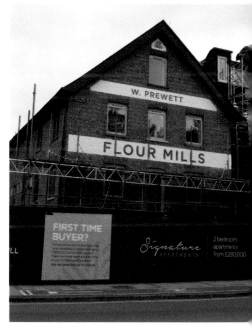

In another twist, Horsham has a link to the Mosley family through Prewett's Mill. The 4th Baronet Mosley (grandfather of Oswald Mosley) had been a pioneer of agriculture, and particularly of wholemeal bread, at his Rolleston bakery. It was the same method of milling wholemeal flour that Prewett's Mill used in its products.

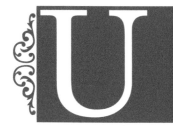

Union Workhouse

The first workhouse was in Normandy from 1727 until 1839, when it moved to a large, purpose-built facility on Crawley Road. The vicar of Horsham purchased the original building for £500 to convert it into St Mary's Almshouses. A more modern building was constructed on the same site in the twentieth century. The replacement workhouse could house up to 250 inmates and in 1899 a separate infirmary block was built beside it. The workhouse continued until 1930, and then became a military hospital during the Second World War, and then a hospital for those with severe learning disabilities from 1948 until 1990. Since then, it has been converted into residential apartments. One of

St Mary's Almshouses, site of Horsham's first workhouse in 1727.

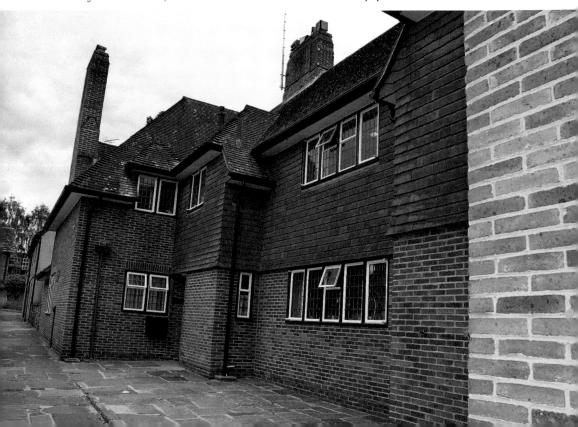

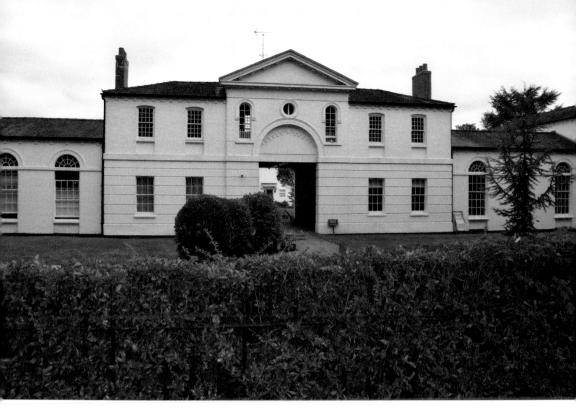

Above: The imposing Union Workhouse in Crawley Road.

Below: The former workhouse infirmary treated VD patients during the Second World War.

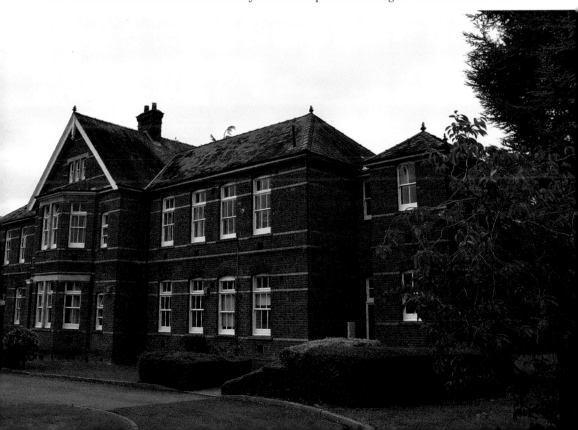

the longest-serving inmates of the original workhouse was a man named Evans, who had spent twenty-two years there when he died on 10 February 1812. He had spent time before then confined in the notorious Bethlem Hospital. His daughter had also spent many years confined in chains at the workhouse due to her mental illness.

In 1830, riots broke out in the town among the workers. They went round the farms demanding food and work. The height of the riots came on 18 November 1830 when 1,000 people armed with pitchforks and sticks forced the town's magistrates to flee to the church. They marched down The Causeway and broke in, threatening to burn the vicar alive. They had already started a fire in Pump Alley (now Talbot Lane, leading from Denne Road to Market Square). More riots started in December 1835 when the guardians forcibly separated inmates and their families: able-bodied adults were to remain at the Normandy workhouse, children were to be sent to Shipley, and the elderly and infirm to Warnham. On 21 December, children from Horsham were removed to Shipley under cover of darkness and on the same day the guardians tried to remove the children from Warnham, but their mothers managed to fight them off.

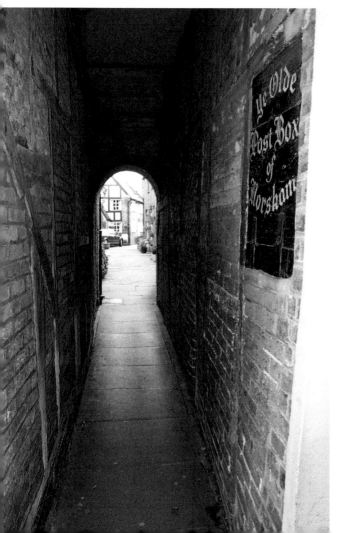

Talbot Lane, formerly Pump Alley, scene of Poor Law riots.

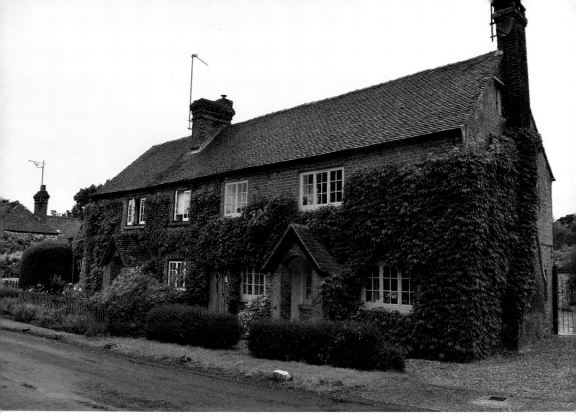

Shipley workhouse, where children were forcibly sent under armed guard in 1835.

On 23 December, a large crowd assembled outside the workhouse and broke up a meeting of the guardians, chasing several of them through the town pelting them with stones and dirt. Sir Charles Burrell had the windows of his carriage smashed and Mr Tredcroft was also attacked. It is said that on one night a gun was fired at the door of the Manor House (Hewells). The main complaint was that reports had come in that the children being sent to Shipley were not being fed properly. The guardians denied this, but Sir Charles Burrell admitted that it was true. On Christmas Eve, the military were drafted in and the children at Warnham were taken from their mothers and loaded onto a wagon that was taken under military escort, swords in hand, through the town to Shipley, along with some elderly women. On Boxing Day, the guardians called on seventy local tradesmen to be drafted as special constables, though only sixty-six turned out, and several of these refused to undertake their orders against the workhouse inmates. The following year it was reported that there were no inmates in the town's workhouse.

A scandal broke in 1880 when a formal complaint was made by the master of the workhouse against the chaplain, Revd J. F. Coles, for cutting a hole in a female inmate's apron. She said that she had received the sacrament from the chaplain when some wine was spilt on her apron. He said that the stained area had been consecrated and he cut it out and deposited it in a box in Roffey Church. More scandals hit in December 1888 when inmates' coffins were not being fitted with handles and were therefore being slid headlong into the graves during the funerals.

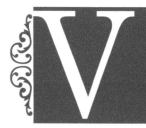

Visitors and Famous Residents

A number of famous feet have graced Horsham's streets over the centuries. Capability Brown was employed to design the gardens of the former Hills house along Guildford Road. The house was demolished long ago and the gardens have all been built on; however, a sole remnant of Brown's work can still (just) be seen today on the footpath outside No. 5 Guildford Road. It is a slab of stone known as Penny Bridge and was a mock bridge built over a stream to hide the view of the road from the gardens.

Captain John Pilfold, a naval commander at the Battle of Trafalgar, was born and baptised at Horsham in 1768. His sister, Elizabeth, married Sir Timothy Shelley, of Field Place, Broadbridge Heath, becoming the parents of the renowned poet, Percy

Penny Bridge, the only remainder of Capability Brown's work in Horsham.

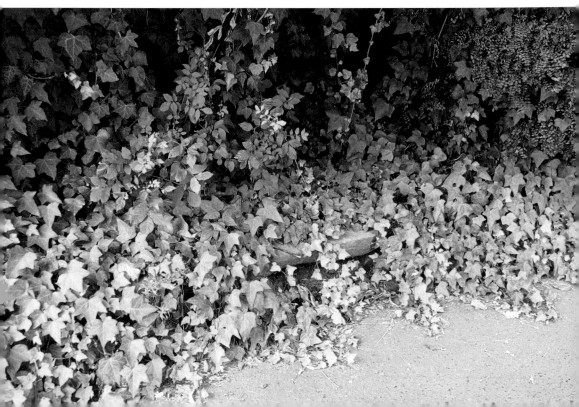

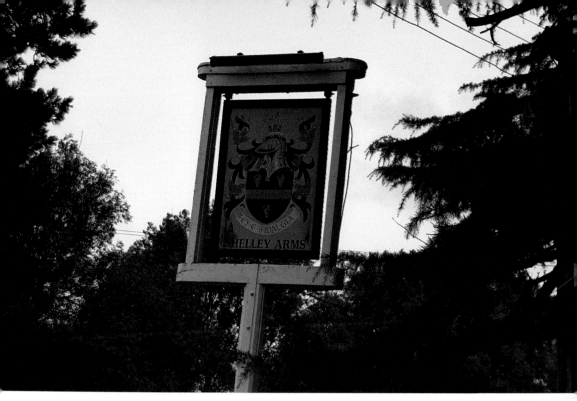

References to Shelley are numerous around Horsham.

Bysshe Shelley. The poet himself was born at Field Place on 4 August 1792 and as a young child would sail model boats on Warnham millpond. He was first taught by the then vicar of Warnham, before leaving the town in 1804 to continue his education. His father, Sir Timothy, had been Horsham's MP from 1790 to 1792. Memorials to members of the Shelley family are found at St Mary's Church.

Barnes Wallis was a student at Christ's Hospital School before having a successful career as an engineer and inventor, most famously of the bouncing bomb. He retained connections to the school well into the 1950s, being on its Council of Almoners. After the war, he was awarded £10,000 for his wartime inventions, which he donated to the families of the men killed on the Dambuster raids and to Christ's Hospital School. Another famous student was Edmund Blunden, the wartime poet.

On 15 October 1931, Cosmo Gordon Lang, Archbishop of Canterbury, visited Horsham to mark the 700th anniversary of Horsham vicarage. On 14 March 2007, Archbishop Rowan Williams visited Christ's Hospital School.

On 23 July 1936, Winston Churchill held a public meeting at Holbrook Park to attack the opposition parties on their stance on rearmament following the German invasion of Czechoslovakia.

In the early 1960s, Neville Duke and his family lived at No. 15 The Causeway, ten years after he gained the world air speed record in 1953. He had become an air ace in the Second World War, with twenty-seven confirmed victories, before becoming a test pilot. His record-breaking Hawker Hunter is on display at Tangmere Museum and a blue plaque was unveiled at his Horsham home on 8 June 2013.

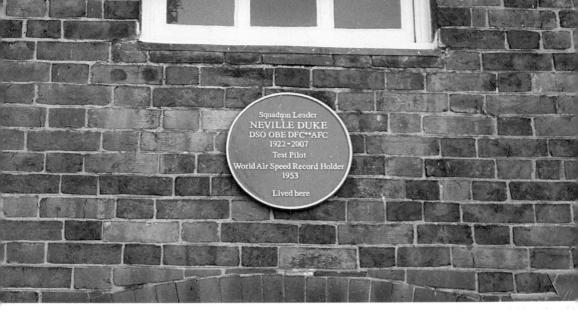

Plaque to Neville Duke at his former home in The Causeway.

On 3 May 1886, Chief Waubuno, of the Delaware Tribe, visited Horsham as the guest of the vicar to address the town's temperance society. He came dressed in his ceremonial costume and headdress. It also happens that his ancestor was the first person to greet William Penn (the former Quaker prisoner at Horsham) when he reached America.

Jomo Kenyatta, who was living and working near Storrington in the 1930s and 40s, addressed two public meetings in Horsham during this time on colonialism and the persecution of black people in Africa. The first was at the Albion Hall (formerly on the site of Swan Walk shopping centre) on 4 February 1939, and again at the town hall on 15 May 1942. He later became the first president of Kenya in 1964. Other foreign visitors were Nana Ofori Atta I, king of Akyem Abuakwa (part of the then Gold Coast Colony), who opened the town's new swimming pool on 11 July 1934. King Leopold III of Belgium had a secret ten-day holiday from 27 December 1935 at Slashers, a house in Broadbridge Heath. Haile Selassie visited Horsham on 31 July 1936 to attend a special session of the Horsham and Crawley Prophetic Convention at the town hall. At the end of his visit he was presented with an Ethiopian cross, which he desired to be displayed at St Mary's Church in memory of his visit. Emir Mai Umar dan Sulayman, ruler of the Bade Emirate in Nigeria, visited Horsham on the weekend of 18 and 19 October 1952 as part of a six-day visit to England to learn more about British local government. He attended several council meetings at the town hall and on 20 October was guest at Christ's Hospital School. Bernardino Machado, president of Portugal, paid a visit to the Roffey Siege School at Roffey Camp on 20 October 1917 to inspect the Portuguese troops stationed there. It was his first visit to the country and, ironically, within seven weeks he was deposed in a military coup and exiled.

A number of British royals have visited Horsham over the years. The first recorded visit was of King Edward I on 12 June 1299 and again on 2 and 3 September, when he stayed at Chesworth House. King Edward II was next to visit on 4 September 1324,

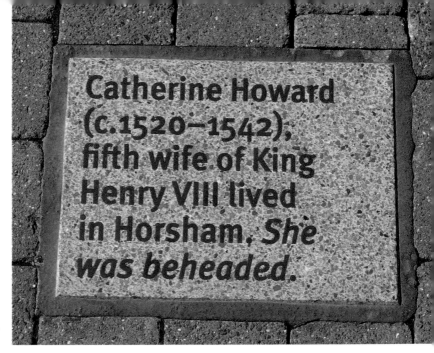

A commemorative plaque to Catherine Howard in West Street.

also staying at Chesworth House. King John is also said to have made the occasional visit to Chesworth. King Henry VII visited in 1488, as did his son King Henry VIII in 1519. Catherine Howard, the ill-fated fifth wife of Henry VIII, lived at Chesworth House as a child in the care of her step-grandmother, Agnes Tilney, wife of the 2nd Duke of Norfolk. The Prince of Wales (later King George III) passed through Horsham on 28 September 1785. Prince Albert Edward (later King Edward VII) stopped at Horsham on 10 May 1876. He visited again on 23 October 1897 to lay the foundation stone of Christ's Hospital School. Prince George, Duke of Cambridge, had already visited the site in May 1896. The body of Queen Victoria passed through Horsham by train on 2 February 1901. Prince Edward (later King Edward VIII) visited Horsham on 19 May 1921 then went on to visit Christ's Hospital School. He visited the school again on 14 October 1930 when he flew in his own personal Gipsy Moth to open a new science building. Queen Mary, consort of King George V, made a number of visits to Leonardslee in the 1930s. In the late 1920s, she made a number of visits to an antiques shop at 6 Market Square. Her last recorded visit was to Roffey Park on 3 July 1946, which at that time was a rehabilitation centre for industrial workers suffering the ill effects of their work. The Duchess of Kent visited on 1 June 1949, first to the Ritz Cinema in North Street (demolished, now the southern-most wing of Spire Court), then to Horsham Hospital in Hurst Road, followed by lunch at the King's Head Hotel and a show at the Court Royal Theatre at No. 28 Carfax (now The Board Game Shop), a trip to the Dedisham children's home at Slinfold, and finally returning to Horsham to inspect the YWCA premises at 10 Market Square. Queen Elizabeth II and the Duke of Edinburgh made their first of two visits on 10 March 1978, when they visited Forest Boys School and the Queen Elizabeth II School. They visited again on 24 October 2003, making stops at Christ's Hospital School, the Capitol Theatre and officially opening The Forum, unveiling the massive sundial sculpture.

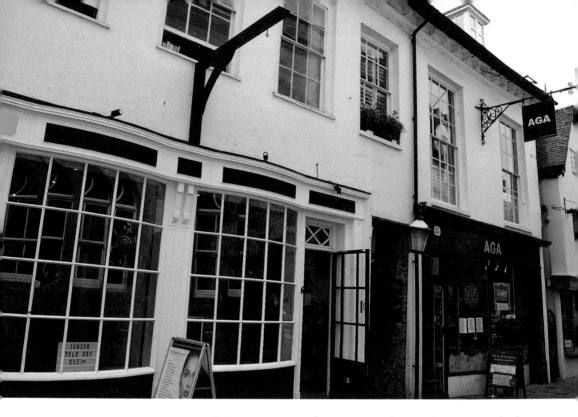

Above: Nos 6 and 10 Market Square – both sites of visits by the Royal Family.

Left: The Court Royal Theatre, which the Duchess of Kent visited in 1949.

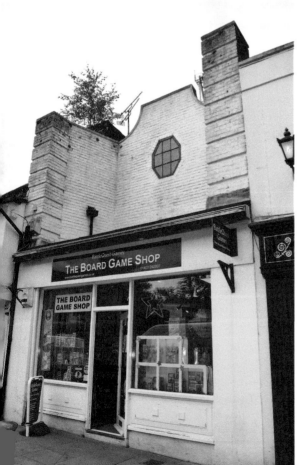

Weird Weather

One of Horsham's claims to fame is holding the record for the largest hailstone. This occurred on 5 September 1958, and the lump of ice weighed over 140 g (some sources say 190 g) and measured 6.35 cm in diameter. Three people were injured by the hailstones, and much damage was done to windows and roof tiles. Oddly, the day had been warm, but at 6.00 p.m. the sky suddenly darkened and masses of ice fell from the clouds. Hail wasn't the only weather to contend with, as severe thunderstorms developed and a mini tornado struck between Southwater and Horsham. A petrol station was one of the victims that was almost completely destroyed. Many chimneys were blown from rooftops and dozens of trees uprooted.

Another mini tornado hit Horsham on 13 October 2004, with winds as high as 100 mph recorded. Like the event of forty-six years previous, chimneys, windows

Plaque in West Street recalling some weird weather.

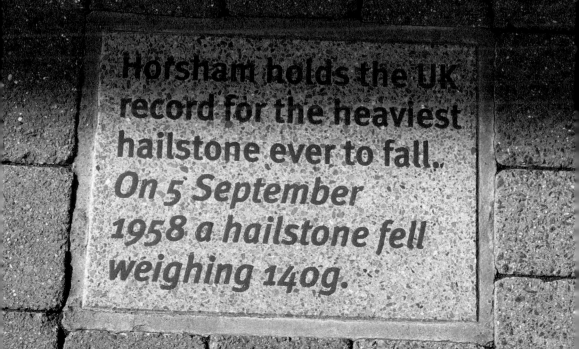

and trees along a half-mile stretch of Brighton Road and Kerves Lane were damaged. Residents are also unlikely to forget the Great Storm of 1987.

In 1810, a severe lightning storm struck, with the house of the town's surgeon, Mr Rickword, being hit, causing extensive damage to the rafters and roof, forcing open all the doors of the house, blowing the oven half way across the kitchen and damaging many metal fixings throughout the house, though remarkably with no injury to the inhabitants. Another house in St Leonard's Forest was struck, knocking unconscious all three of the women inside. Large hailstones were also reported during the storm.

A snow storm on 26 December 1886 also created havoc, with a large drift trapping many people in their homes and bringing down telegraph wires. The Arun also overflowed, flooding the churchyard and Prewett's Mill, and demolishing a bridge. A bakers in Queen Street was flooded to a depth of 4 feet. Many livestock in the district were killed, either from the cold or from the floods. Arctic conditions had previously been experienced in the winter of 1837/38 when wine froze solid and pieces of ice floated in the air. The following winter was a report of what today would be called ball-lightning floating a few feet in the air, as well as large hailstones 2.5 inches across (clearly Horsham is no stranger to unusually large hailstones!) In 1945, the temperatures in the town fell to −19 °C.

Storms, tornadoes and record-breaking hail are not the only weird weather that Horsham has experienced. On 31 March 1832, a small earthquake shook the town, causing much concern among the population, but no damage. On 2 April 1833, another small earthquake struck. Another one struck on 8 December 1930, with reports from the town, Broadbridge Heath and Coolham. On 8 September 1937, another earthquake hit and was strong enough to shake houses, move furniture and cause objects to fall. On 16 July 2005, another small earthquake, and several aftershocks were felt around the Horsham District, particularly in the Billingshurst area. More recently, media was again excited by a 2.7 magnitude earthquake that struck the West Sussex–Surrey border on 1 April 2018, with some residents of Horsham reporting having felt the tremors just after midday. A larger 3.0 magnitude earthquake was felt in Horsham on 5 July, causing some desks and furniture to move. This was part of a series of earthquakes in the Newdigate area that had been occurring since April.

Although not weather related, on 8 February 1812, Horsham residents were exposed to a 'tremulous agitation of the air, or earth, or both' which vexed any attempts for an explanation for several hours, until news reached the town that a powder mill at Ewell – some 20 miles away – had exploded.

Witchcraft

There were eight recorded cases of witchcraft at Horsham between 1577 and 1680. Writing in 1929, C. L'Estrange Ewen recorded the first two cases at Horsham on 8 July 1577: those of Margery Barrowe and Juliana Curtis. Alice Casselowe was tried at

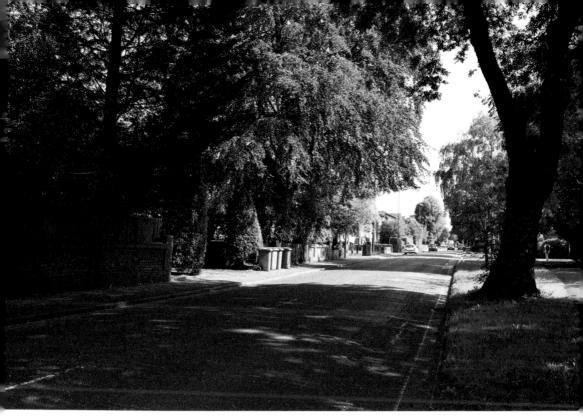

Here in Kings Road is where witches and criminals were originally hanged.

Horsham in 1577 for bewitching an ox and two pigs to death. She was found guilty and sentenced to one year in gaol, where she died. Ewen also records a case in 1579, that of Alice Stedman. The only male accused was Richard Luckins, the town gaoler, who was charged with, among other things, employing the services of witches to track down escaped prisoners. He appears to have been acquitted, since he seems to have kept his job. Jane Shoubridge was tried at Horsham in July 1654 for bewitching Mary Muddle, aged twelve, and Clement Shoubridge was tried at the same assizes for bewitching Benjamin Caught and Mary Muddle. Both women (presumably sisters, or mother and daughter) were acquitted. The final case was of Alice Nash in July 1680, who was accused of bewitching and causing the deaths of Elizabeth Slater, aged two, and Anne Slater, aged five. She, too, was acquitted.

At least three other witch trials took place at East Grinstead between 1572 and 1692, and owing to Horsham's role as county gaol and place of execution, it is possible that the sentences were carried out here.

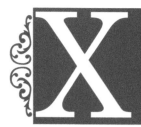

X-Files: Horsham's Own Paranormal Encounters

The town is no stranger to ghostly sightings. St Leonard's Forest is particularly well known for its 'poisonous dragon', and more recently for another strange creature that is never seen but can be heard rustling through the tree canopy. It is also haunted by a headless horseman, said to be the ghost of Captain Paulett. Dragons and large serpents appear to be a phenomenon unique to western Sussex, with many legends about snakes dating back centuries. In 1809, a young pregnant woman from Horsham

Can you spot the unicorn and tree-dweller on the sundial?

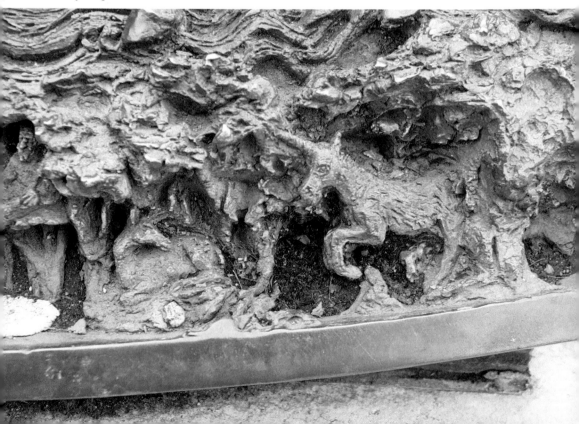

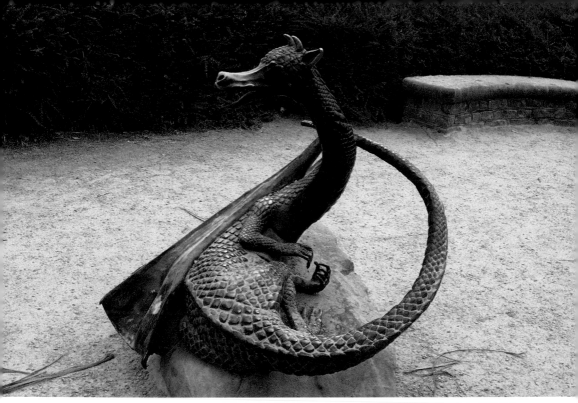

Above: The infamous St Leonard's Dragon in Horsham Park.

Right: The Causeway, scene of Horsham's most well-known haunting.

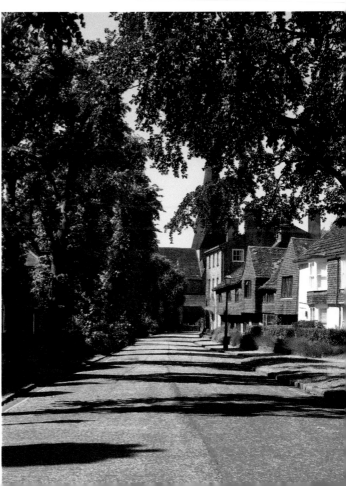

was gathering nuts nearby when she was bitten on the ankle by an adder, before being chased by a second across the field. She sadly miscarried, but otherwise made a full recovery from the bite. She had been with another woman in whom the snakes showed no interest, and it was a legend in the county that adders would always pick out pregnant women in a crowd.

An old farmhouse at Rickfield Farm, between Horsham and Mannings Heath, was left empty for many years in the early twentieth century due to the occupants being plagued by strange noises and banging on doors. The Causeway and churchyard have had repeated sightings of ghostly figures. The first is said to wander down The Causeway before disappearing when reaching the churchyard gates. The other, a monk, emanates from the church crypt before disappearing when he gets to the vicarage wall.

A number of UFO sightings have been reported over the years. In 1976, a long, rod-shaped craft with flashing lights was spotted above the town, and orange lights were spotted in the skies in 2008 and twice in 2011. The MoD recorded two UFO sightings, both in 1998. The first, on 9 August, was of an object with three flashing lights, and the other, on 12 December, was of a single, bright, circular white light that moved across the sky. More recently, on 23 October 2012, a number of Horsham residents reported hearing a pulsating sound circling the town at night, loud enough to wake many people and for the vibrations to be felt. Another was spotted over the weekend of 1–2 February 2014, said to have been a round object in the sky. On 24 July 2015 a large crop circle appeared off the Rusper Road a few miles north of Horsham.

The dragon is also hidden on the sundial sculpture in The Forum.

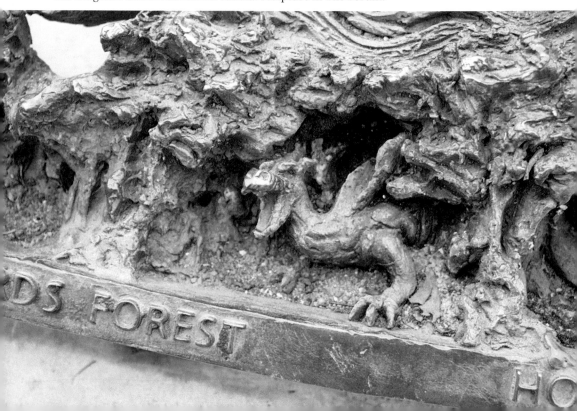

Y

Ye Old King's Head

Hidden behind an eighteenth-century façade is a much older building, which, along with the adjacent building, has played a central role in much of Horsham's history. In addition to its role as a hotel, the building has hosted stables, a post office, assembly rooms (which once was home to the Brighton Road Baptist Church), wine merchants, Inland Revenue Office, a Masonic lodge, Oddfellows meeting house, an omnibus office and a car garage, and is now a restaurant. It was at the assembly rooms that, in 1863, the churchwardens cracked down on seventeen town residents and tradesmen who refused to pay the church tax and seized their belongings to auction them off. No Horsham auctioneer would be part of this, and the churchwardens had to engage the services of one from Brighton. Aside from the particular act of seizing property to auction, it was the severity of the seizures that particularly attracted attention: one person had thirteen pairs of boots worth £8 7s 6d taken for a debt of just 5s 6d, another lost an £8 carpet to pay a 7s debt, with a third person being deprived of £5 worth of items.

In early December 1784, the remains of Catherine Howard, Duchess of Norfolk, laid in state at the King's Head for several days en route to being buried at Arundel. The coffin was draped in crimson velvet.

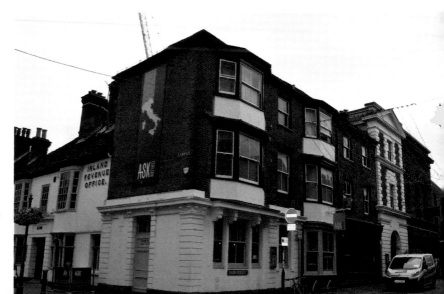

The King's Head, now an Italian restaurant.

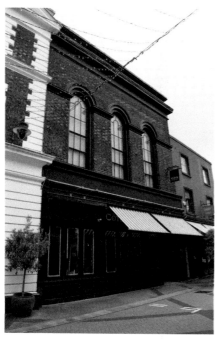

Left: The Assembly Rooms, scene of many historic moments.

Below: The oldest part of Ye Old King's Head.

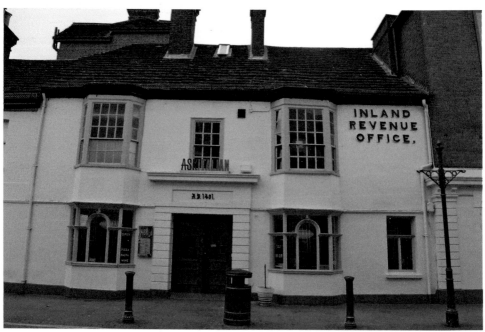

It was also at the King's Head car park that a Messerschmitt Me 109 was put on public display in 1941 to raise funds for the town to purchase its own Spitfire. A Heinkel He 111 was also originally intended for display at the King's Head, but it was too large and was instead displayed in Springfield Road.

Z

Zany Buildings

Sometimes architects think outside the box. Here are some of the more 'zany' experiments of modern architecture that can be found in town.

St John's Church, Broadbridge Heath

Opened in the early 1960s after replacing an older Edwardian church, its pyramid-like shape consists of four large triangular vertical façades, joined at the centre and tiled down to ground level between each triangle. It is certainly a unique design, nestled within the residential streets of Broadbridge Heath.

Law Courts, Hurst Road

Perhaps one of the least attractive buildings that can be found in Horsham, the law courts were clearly designed for function rather than appearance. Resembling a kind of modern-day castle, visitors cross a bridge over the 'moat' (the car park), through a gateway bearing a large royal coat of arms and into a central courtyard. Behind the courts is the police station, which moved here from Barttelot Road. The current station retains the red lantern from the old station.

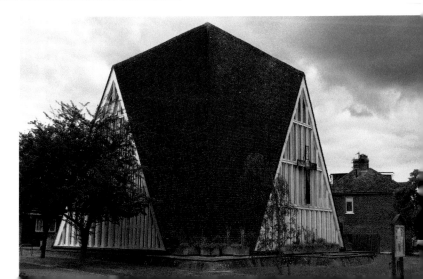

St John's Church,
Broadbridge Heath.

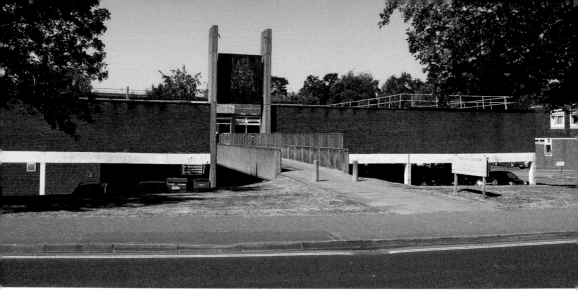

The Law Courts in Hurst Road. A modern castle?

West Point, Springfield Road

Perhaps one of the most unusual buildings in Horsham, along with St John's Church at Broadbridge Heath, West Point is certainly a statement piece in the centre of town. Each floor of its five storeys is rotated at 45° to the one below, creating a star-shaped profile from above. Even the stairwell on the southern side of the building includes this offset design of each floor, resembling a Jenga block tower. West Point is definitely a unique feature on Horsham's landscape.

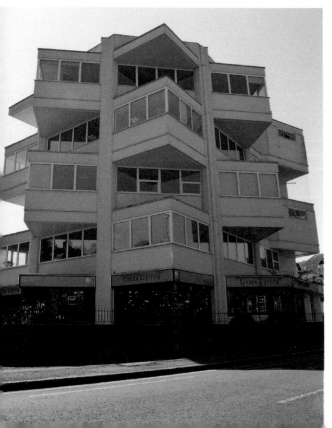

West Point, Springfield Road.